TRAVEL REPORT

An APPRENTICESHIP *in the* EARL *of* DERBY'S
KITCHEN GARDENS *and* GREENHOUSES
at KNOWSLEY, ENGLAND

ex horto

DUMBARTON OAKS TEXTS
IN GARDEN AND LANDSCAPE STUDIES

In cooperation with the Center of Garden Art and Landscape Architecture
Leibniz University of Hannover

TRAVEL REPORT

An APPRENTICESHIP *in the* EARL *of* DERBY'S KITCHEN GARDENS *and* GREENHOUSES *at* KNOWSLEY, ENGLAND

HANS JANCKE,
author

JOACHIM WOLSCHKE-BULMAHN,
editor

MIC HALE,
translator

DUMBARTON OAKS RESEARCH LIBRARY AND COLLECTION
WASHINGTON, D.C.

Library of Congress Cataloging-in-Publication Data

    Jancke, Hans, 1850–1920.

    [Reise-Bericht. English]

    Travel report: an apprenticeship in the Earl of Derby's kitchen gardens and greenhouses at Knowsley, England / Hans Jancke, author; Joachim Wolschke-Bulmahn, editor; Mic Hale, translator. — 1st English ed.

       p. cm. — (Ex Horto: Dumbarton Oaks texts in garden and landscape studies)

    Translation of: Reise-Bericht, originally published in 1875.

    Includes bibliographical references.

      ISBN 978-0-88402-389-0 (alk. paper)

    1. Gardens—England—Knowsley. 2. Knowsley Hall (England).

    3. Knowsley (England). 4. Derby, Edward Henry Stanley, Earl of, 1826–1893.

    I. Wolschke-Bulmahn, Joachim. II. Dumbarton Oaks. III. Title.

    IV. Title: Apprenticeship in the Earl of Derby's kitchen gardens and greenhouses at Knowsley, England. V. Series: Ex Horto: Dumbarton Oaks texts in garden and landscape studies.

    SB451.36.G7J3613 2013

    635.09427'54—dc23

                 2013009213

Series editor: John Beardsley

Managing editor: Sara Taylor

Series design: Melissa Tandysh

Frontispiece: Hans Oskar Jancke. Hans Oskar Jancke Papers, Stiftung Preußische Schlösser und Gärten Berlin-Brandenburg (SPSG), F0019313. (Photograph: Daniel Lindner)

Published in collaboration with the Center of Garden Art and Landscape Architecture (CGL), Leibniz University of Hannover.

www.doaks.org/publications

CONTENTS

FOREWORD

$\mathcal{T}$his volume presents a full transcription and translation of a very unusual handwritten manuscript in the Rare Book Collection at Dumbarton Oaks by the nineteenth-century German court gardener Hans Jancke. The manuscript is a journal of Jancke's extended stay at Knowsley, the seat of the Earl of Derby near Liverpool, in 1874–75. At the time, Knowsley possessed an extensive landscaped park along with comprehensive facilities for the cultivation of indigenous and exotic ornamental plants, fruits, and vegetables, which were the particular focus of Jancke's lengthy and detailed report and its illustrations.

Jancke (1850–1920) was born into German garden culture, as his father was the secretary of the great Prussian garden designer Peter Joseph Lenné. Jancke himself would be one of the last pupils of Gustav Meyer, the most influential successor of Lenné. He ultimately became a court gardener at Potsdam-Sanssouci, where he also taught plan drawing and surveying at the Royal Gardeners Institute. After 1884, he was royal master gardener at Bellevue in Berlin.

Educational journeys, such as the one Jancke took to Knowsley, were an important part of a gardener's training throughout the nineteenth century. They often resulted in elaborate reports and articles for professional publications; Jancke's journal is a particularly good example of this genre. But such travel literature is seldom studied. Given how little is known in particular about the trips to England made by Lenné and his associates, the present publication—which makes Jancke's manuscript more widely available—marks a significant contribution to garden studies. The wealth of information about the plants under cultivation at Knowsley will be of great value to botanists and garden historians, and the descriptions and drawings of the greenhouses will be of particular interest to historians of technology.

Jancke's manuscript—a thin, reddish-brown notebook measuring 34.3 × 21.7 cm and consisting of 122 numbered pages, with four sheets of ink and watercolor illustrations at the back—was acquired for the Rare Book Collection at Dumbarton Oaks from the London antiquarian bookshop Marlborough Rare

Books Ltd. in 1995, when Joachim Wolschke-Bulmahn was director of Garden and Landscape Studies. Its transcription and translation have been a joint project of Dumbarton Oaks and the Center of Garden Art and Landscape Architecture (CGL) at Leibniz University of Hannover, where Professor Wolschke-Bulmahn is now director. Dumbarton Oaks is pleased to collaborate with the CGL on this project, which furthers our joint commitment to advanced scholarship in garden history and landscape architecture.

JOHN BEARDSLEY
Director, Garden and Landscape Studies
Dumbarton Oaks

ACKNOWLEDGMENTS

*I*n conducting research on the gardener Hans Jancke and his travel report, I received valuable support and assistance from a variety of people and institutions. I would like to take this opportunity to thank the Stiftung Preußische Schlösser und Gärten Berlin-Brandenburg (SPSG) foundation and its director, Michael Rohde, who drew my attention to Jancke's papers in the SPSG archives; and Ms. Karla Camara and Ms. M. Tretter, who ensured ideal working conditions in the foundation archives and made it possible to obtain reproductions of important objects in the Hans Oskar Jancke Papers.

I thank Peter Goodchild and David Jacques for their observations on Knowsley. My gratitude goes also to John Edmondson, for offering information about Knowsley and for providing important publications, and to Ms. Kirstin Waibel, then curator of collections at the Derby Collection Image Library, Knowsley, who made available Anna Sholl's "The Historical Development of Knowsley Park" and other material. Her successor at Knowsley, Stephen Lloyd, also supported the project. A particular thank you is due to Brent Elliott and Mark Laird. Brent Elliott supplied me with articles from various horticultural magazines about Knowsley and offered me his expertise on the significance of Knowsley for nineteenth-century horticulture. Mark Laird supported this project from the very beginning; his most important contribution was his excellent comments on an earlier draft of the introductory essay.

Mic Hale excellently translated the transcription of the travel report into English. Thanks also to Linda Lott, rare book librarian at Dumbarton Oaks, for supporting my work, to Joe Mills for supplying the illustrations of the travel report, and to Michael Lee and Anatole Tchikine for their excellent editorial work on the transcription of the travel report. I would like to thank Patrick Kruse, who, as my student assistant at the Institut für Landschaftsarchitektur, made a painstaking transcript of the Jancke manuscript, and to Isabel David, for her excellent proofreading of the first version of the transcription. Sara Taylor and Kathy Sparkes, from the publications office at Dumbarton Oaks, deserve a thank you for their important contributions in publishing the work.

I am particularly grateful to Jan Ziolkowski, director of Dumbarton Oaks, and John Beardsley, director of Garden and Landscape Studies at Dumbarton Oaks, for giving the Center of Garden Art and Landscape Architecture (CGL) of Leibniz University of Hannover the honor and pleasure of collaborating on such a fascinating publication.

JOACHIM WOLSCHKE-BULMAHN
Center of Garden Art
and Landscape Architecture
Leibniz University of Hannover

INTRODUCTION

JOACHIM WOLSCHKE-BULMAHN

*F*or centuries, travel was an important part of a gardener's or garden artist's initial and continuing professional training. From the Renaissance onward, the Grand Tour led the nobility and members of the educated middle class to such places as Italy, Greece, Spain, and the Holy Land.[1] Later—with the flourishing of the landscape garden, the rise of industrialization, and the development of agriculture—Great Britain became a favored destination for German elites and even more so for professional gardeners and garden designers.[2]

The international allure of gardening—even in times of a powerful national, indeed, nationalistic zeitgeist such as that which prevailed in Germany during the *Kaiserreich* (1871–1918)—was striking.[3] In the second half of the nineteenth century, the major commercial nurseries of Europe—Belgian firms such as Van Houtte, Makoy, Verschaffelt, and Linden, or the Veitch Nurseries in England—were highly sought out as places of learning by aspiring German gardeners, horticulturists, and landscape designers, especially those in the early stages of their careers.[4] And again, England in particular was a preeminent destination. This precedence may be demonstrated by reference to the Veitch firm alone, where many German gardeners spent the formative part of their careers in the late nineteenth century. During the nineteenth century, the Veitch Nurseries were the largest group of family-run plant nurseries in Europe. For example, Heinrich Brasch—who trained at the Königliche Gärtnerlehranstalt Wildpark-Potsdam and was later appointed Königlicher Obergärtner at Sanssouci, Charlottenburg, and Brühl (after 1904)—went to the commercial nurseries of Fisher Son & Sibray, near Sheffield, in 1884–85 (after two years employment at Berggarten in Hannover) and James Veitch & Sons, Chelsea, London, in 1885.[5] Garteninspektor Viktor Buchholz, who was employed by the Botanischer Garten Hamburg from 1933 to 1937, was at Kew Gardens, then went on to work at the botanic gardens in Cambridge and at Veitch & Sons (from 1910 to 1914).[6] Hans Johann Karl Heins

was an assistant at the Veitch & Sons tree nursery in Coombe Wood, London, for several months in 1907–8.[7] Rudolf Wilhelm Hermann Lauche, the Parkdirektor at Muskau until 1928, worked for eighteen months in 1881–82 at Veitch & Sons and at the royal gardens at Windsor.[8] Garteninspektor Karl Bernhard Lebrun was an assistant in 1879 at Kew Gardens and at Veitch & Sons.[9] Friedrich Wilhelm Meyer went to England in 1874 after three years in Belgium and France; he subsequently stayed for around twenty-five years as garden architect and landscape gardener at Robert Veitch & Sons in Exeter.[10] Even the tree nursery proprietor Hellmuth Ludwig Späth underwent six months of practical training at the Veitch Nurseries in London in 1907.

Foreign excursions were also for the royal gardeners (*Hofgärtner*) an essential element of horticultural "initial and further training, and the basis for collegial pan-European exchange."[11] So that royal gardeners possessed the latest and most advanced methods, traveling to foreign gardens as a means of professional self-improvement was considered crucial, and the practice was held in very high regard. Such esteem may be inferred from the documents in which Hans Jancke (Figures 1 and 2) submitted a request to Wilhelm I for an increase in their remuneration:

figure 2

Hans Jancke with
Elisabeth and Rose.

Hans Oskar Jancke Papers,
Stiftung Preußische
Schlösser und Gärten
Berlin-Brandenburg
(spsg), F0019311.
(Photograph:
Daniel Lindner)

"Duke Keller emphasized, in a suit from Jancke addressed to Wilhelm I on 29 May 1876 concerning a rise in the royal gardeners' wages: 'It is expected of the royal gardeners that they undergo professional training involving expensive journeys and passing an examination in order to meet the requirements of modern gardening; they are furthermore to be counted as members of the more highly educated circles of society, namely in that many are reserve or militia officers. I thus consider it unjustifiable to rank them with the palace chatelaines, on whom no such requirements are placed."[12] Jancke himself made several travels to broaden his horticultural knowledge—the most important being his stay in Knowsley, near Liverpool, in 1874–75 to study its horticultural enterprises.

But royal gardeners having their educational expeditions financed by their employers seems to have been the exception, not the rule, and it appears to have been granted to "but a few outstanding gardeners."[13] For example, an account of the royal gardeners at Potsdam-Sanssouci relates: "Apart from Lenné, the privilege of educational journeys was granted only to the royal gardeners Hermann and Emil Sello. Hermann Sello travelled, for purposes unknown, to St. Petersburg in 1851. Through the exceptional generosity shown by the Crown Prince and his

consort, Emil Sello could travel as royal gardener to London, Paris and Vienna, of which journeys he completed meticulous accounts for his sovereign."[14]

These gardeners' and garden artists' educational excursions to parks and gardens at home and abroad were consistently recorded in lengthy and detailed reports and articles for professional journals. (Jancke himself wrote a 122-page report after he finished his stay at Knowsley.) Such travel reports were long ignored as reputable sources for specialist historical research. But as eyewitness testimony that provides information about the history of the garden arts and horticulture, they have tremendous potential. An excellent example is the report by Hans Jancke on his study journey to England. Jancke spent a considerable amount of time at Knowsley, the seat of the Earl of Derby near Liverpool, in 1874–75. At the time of Jancke's stay, Knowsley possessed an admirable park in the landscape style as well as comprehensive facilities for the cultivation of ornamental plants, fruits, and vegetables. Jancke compiled a lengthy and detailed description of his experience there.

Hans Jancke, Biographical Remarks

Hans Jancke, the son of Peter Joseph Lenné's secretary, was born in 1850. He began his career in the Melonerie at Sanssouci. In 1868 and 1869, he was one of the last

figure 4

Royal gardener's home at Georgengarten in Hannover.

Hans Oskar Jancke Papers, Stiftung Preußische Schlösser und Gärten Berlin-Brandenburg (SPSG), 1550/184, F0019312. (Photograph: Daniel Lindner)

pupils of Gustav Meyer (1816–77) at the Königliche Gärtnerlehranstalt Wildpark-
Potsdam (Figure 3). In Theodor Echtermeyer's memoir on the Königliche
Gärtnerlehranstalt Dahlem,[15] the brief biographies of graduates from the garden-
ing academies at Wildpark-Potsdam and Berlin-Dahlem include the following
details about Jancke's career: after his employment with Borsig in Moabit, Simon
Louis Freres in Metz, Linden in Ghent, and his stay at Knowsley, he worked at
the Georgengarten in Hannover (Figure 4) and at the Neuer Garten in Potsdam.
From 1880 to 1884, he was a teacher at the Königliche Gärtnerlehranstalt in
Sanssouci. From 1884 onward, he was Königlicher Oberhofgärtner at Bellevue in
Berlin. Jancke received numerous honors.[16] On the occasion of an exhibition by

the Königliche Garten-Intendantur zu Potsdam, he was presented with an honorary diploma for the "plants provided in exquisite culture" (Figure 5). A collection of thirty-two visiting cards—including those by "members of the gardener dynasties of Fintelmann, Nietner, Jancke and Sello, along with those of Ferdinand Jühlke and 'Madame F. Lenné'"—in the Hans Oskar Jancke Papers bears witness to the highly respected social standing of this royal gardener.[17] Jancke died on February 11, 1920, in Potsdam.[18]

The following sections will discuss why Jancke went to Knowsley and what he could have learned and experienced there regarding horticulture and garden culture.

Knowsley and the Earls of Derby

In nineteenth-century England, Knowsley was an important stately home with a tradition going back centuries (Figure 6).[19] In the eighteenth and nineteenth centuries especially, its owners, the Earls of Derby, appear to have taken—to varying degrees—a lively interest in the design of the park grounds, the breeding of exotic animals, the creation of suitable enclosures and menageries, and the cultivation of plants, particularly fruit trees and orchids.

Lancelot Brown (1716–83) likely impacted the design of the park. The Garden History Society related the following during its 2008 conference in Liverpool:

> As Knowsley assumed a more prominent role, and after 1660 became the principal seat, it was embellished architecturally and its park was subject to successive phases of landscaping. The park itself is one of the largest in Britain, first mentioned in 1292. . . . The dominant element in the "public" areas of the park (a misnomer, since it is strictly private) is of the mid-eighteenth century, when extensive remodelling was undertaken under the influence or (according to some sources) direct work of Lancelot Brown. However, the greater part of the park was substantially reshaped in the early nineteenth century when a model Home Farm and other agricultural projects were undertaken by the improvement-minded twelfth and thirteenth earls.[20]

It is worth noting that Knowsley is mentioned only in passing, if at all, in several monographs on Lancelot Brown.[21] It may then be assumed that Brown's plans were not executed—or at least not to any substantial degree.[22]

Probably the most comprehensive study of the gardens at Knowsley was published by Anna Sholl for the Groundwork Trust in 1985 under the title *The Historical Development of Knowsley Park: A Study of the Landscape, 1085–1985*.[23] Sholl also associates Lancelot Brown and William Gilpin with the development of the parkland without unequivocally affirming their direct involvement.[24] Reference to the

South Elevation, Knowsley Hall.

figure 6

South elevation of
Knowsley Hall, from
J. H. D., "Knowsley
Hall," supplement to the
Journal of Horticulture
(March 3, 1910): 187.

horticultural importance of Knowsley as a place for the propagation of fruit trees, shrubs, and ornamental plants, especially under the thirteenth and fourteenth Earls of Derby, is rather limited.[25]

The Thirteenth Earl of Derby

The thirteenth Earl of Derby, Edward Smith Stanley, formerly Lord Stanley (1775–1851), a politician and naturalist, played a leading role in the introduction and breeding of animals as well as in the introduction of exotic plants. Lord Stanley was a Whig member of parliament, and "[t]hroughout his parliamentary career he was a firm and consistent supporter of the Whig party without ever taking a prominent place in it."[26] After succeeding his father to the earldom in 1834, Derby "played little part in political life, but became increasingly prominent in the world of natural history, especially as one of the figureheads of the science of zoological classification, particularly the taxonomy of birds. He was president of the Linnean

Society of London from 1828 to 1834, and president of the Zoological Society of London for twenty years from 1831 until his death."[27] At Knowsley, he established an "extensive menagerie of birds and mammals. His record of keeping and breeding rare and later extinct species of bird is still regarded as extraordinary; he was the first to breed in captivity such species as the nene (or Hawaiian goose) and the passenger pigeon . . . At his death the living collections included 345 mammals of 94 species (principally antelopes); of these, no fewer than 207 individuals of 39 species had been bred at Knowsley. His aviaries contained 1,272 birds of 318 species."[28] A contemporary author for *The Gardeners' Chronicle* commented in 1841 that besides having a desire "to possess living animals for the elucidation of the science of Natural History," Derby wanted to introduce "such animals as are likely to become useful either as food or to furnish materials for manufacturing purposes."[29] The author also emphasized Derby's special interest in orchids and praised "his excellent collection," which might have been attributed "to the exertions of his Lordship's collectors, who are in various parts of the world, and from time to time keep transmitting to Knowsley what Orchidaceae they may deem valuable."[30] In the *Journal of Horticulture and Home Farmer,*[31] the thirteenth Earl is characterized "from a horticultural standpoint" as "pre-eminently notable" and his contributions to plant expeditions are emphasized.[32]

The importance of the greenhouses and the cultivation of exotic decorative plants, fruit trees, and shrubs in the Knowsley gardens during the thirteenth Earl's stewardship appear to have merited international attention, as, for example, the extensive mention of Knowsley in *A Dictionary of Modern Gardening* (1847 [Philadelphia]) attests. Under the "orangery" entry, the Knowsley greenhouse construction is presented as an exemplary model: "ORANGERY is a green-house or conservatory devoted to the cultivation of the genus *Citrus*: The best plan for the construction of such a building is that erected at Knowsley Park, and thus described by the gardener, Mr. J. W. Jones."[33] Following the entry is an account of the construction of the greenhouse, the type and construction of the planting frames, the heating system and other details of the forcing houses; a section and plan provide further information. Reference is also made to exceptional plants and the way they are cultivated in the orangery: "The oranges, citrons &., are all trained as espaliers. . . . In this some fine climbing plants have been turned out amongst which are several plants of *Passiflora quadrangularis*, which bear an abundant crop of fine fruit. Besides these, there are also two fine plants of the beautiful new *Gardenia Sherbournia*."[34]

Another detailed account of Knowsley during the time of the thirteenth Earl may be found in *The Gardeners' Chronicle* of 1841:

> The gardens at Knowsley are very extensive, particularly the forcing and kitchen departments: the kitchen-garden contains about seven statute

acres, and is enclosed by a high wall and belt of trees: it is divided by two hot walls, running longitudinally from east to west; the walls of the kitchen-garden are well stocked with Peach, Nectarine, Plum, Apricot, Cherry, and the finer sorts of Pear trees; the soil of the kitchen-garden is a stiff wet loam; it is, however capable of producing good crops. The kitchen-garden is divided into four quarters; in the centre of each is a circular pond, from which the garden is supplied with water in dry weather. The forcing department may be considered as very extensive, there being a great quantity of Grapes, Peaches, Cherries, Figs, Pine-apples, Melons, and Cucumbers grown; besides the forcing-houses used in growing these fruits, there are several ranges of pits used for growing Melons and culinary vegetables. The ornamental department is likewise very extensive, with the exception of the flower-garden: however, a new one is now in progress. There is a good collection of Cape, Bulbs, Stove, Greenhouse, and Orchidaceous plants; it may be said the latter is a very choice one— The Earl of Derby is very partial to Orchidaceae, and his excellent collection may be attributed in a great measure to the exertions of his Lordship's collectors, who are in various parts of the world, and from time to time keep transmitting to Knowsley what Orchidaceae they may deem valuable. The greenhouse is a large but old edifice well stocked with plants; it is now in contemplation to have it removed and supplanted by a large conservatory.[35]

A Social Critic's View of Knowsley at the Time of the Thirteenth Earl

Not just those who were concerned with horticulture and gardens took an interest in Knowsley. Alexander Somerville (1811–85) was a Scottish radical journalist and soldier who focused not on zoology or horticulture but on social and political realities during his travels through England. *The Whistler at the Plough and Free Trade* (1852) was the result of Somerville's socially critical approach in which he also considered Knowsley.[36] His most pungent criticism was addressed to the excessive enclosure of the land and the waste of arable land through other measures. He criticized the Corn Laws and championed the rights of the rural population. But on the Knowsley Park itself, his book adopts a thoroughly positive tone:

> My Lord, a word about Knowsley Park. You could not fail to observe last summer the splendid crops of potatoes and Swedish turnips that grew on each side of the approach to the Hall from the Liverpool Road. You are aware, perhaps, that the preparing of the soil for the seed, with the summer clearing of the crops, was done in a different manner from the common style of working in Lancashire. You must, doubtless, know that the

soil was previously sour, wet, and profitless, and that your noble father has allowed the Tweedside ploughmen, who within these last few years have been brought to Knowsley, to break up portions of the vast park that surrounds the ancient hall of your forefathers, for the purpose of improving the soil, to be again laid down in permanent grass.... Knowing those circumstances, the improvements made and still making in Knowsley Park, the splendid crops raised from a formerly unproductive soil, your Lordship must also well know that the Tweedside system of working is superior to the Lancashire system. But it can never be introduced to the Knowsley estate beyond the bounds of Knowsley Park, *unless the tenants obtain leases....* You are aware, my Lord, that the cultivators of the soil of New South Wales must have security in their property. Why then withhold it from the tenants of Knowsley?[37]

Here, then, one finds in Somerville, some time before Jancke traveled to Knowsley, a very frank social critic of the plight of the country people of England and the specific situation at Knowsley. Jancke did not comment on the situation of the local rural population, which perhaps had changed little by the time of his visit. And Jancke did not devote too much time to Knowsley as a landscape park.[38]

Knowsley during the Time of the Thirteenth Earl as a Garden for the Acclimatization of Animals

During the thirteenth Earl's stewardship, Knowsley was a key place for the importation and breeding of exotic animals. Gardens and parks as locations for animal enclosures and menageries are often the subject of garden history research.[39] In connection with Knowsley, the studies by Sally Festing, "Menageries and the Landscape Garden," and Mark Laird, "This Other Eden: The American Connection in Georgian Pleasure Grounds, from Shrubbery and Menagerie to Aviary and Flower Garden," stand out. Festing draws on examples from numerous English country estates and landscape gardens to describe the importance of menageries and the keeping of exotic animals.[40] "Foreign animals" seem to have become a status symbol in the eighteenth century: "some menagerie owners were passionately interested ornithologists and natural historians."[41] Along with William Chambers, Lancelot Brown is also mentioned, among other garden artists, as one of the "menagerie proponent[s]." Festing declares that "by mid-century, animals were almost as important a part of the landscape setting as plants."[42] She goes on to say that "menageries continued to be popular in the nineteenth century and later collections are much better documented."[43] Knowsley can probably be included in this development. Even so, with regard to the quality of its collection of exotic animals in mid-nineteenth-century England, it seems to have been exceptional. Mark Laird has discussed "how flora and fauna, exotic and indigenous, came together in Georgian pleasure grounds."[44] Knowsley during the time of the thirteenth Earl of Derby might be seen as an example for this concurrence to the Victorian period.

Knowsley's prominent role in the world of zoology is confirmed by contemporary accounts from Germany. The scientific secretary of the Zoologische Gesellschaft and Doctor for Zoology at Senckenbergisches Museum in Frankfurt am Main, D. F. Weinland, concurrently editor of the journal *Der Zoologische Garten: Organ für die Zoologische Gesellschaft Frankfurt am Main*, published in 1860 a prescriptive article entitled "Was ein Zoologischer Garten leisten soll" (What a Zoological Garden Should Be Capable Of).[45] He saw one of the three crucial responsibilities as acclimatization, a task that botanical gardens had long been systematically addressing with regard to plants. He himself referred to the "old Jardin des Plantes in Paris which, originally mainly a menagerie, later gradually but never completely evolved into the epitome of a zoological garden."[46] Very similar to the acclimatization of plants, animal acclimatization was primarily conceived by Weinland as "the adaptation of the animal to our climate or acclimatisation in the narrower sense."[47] The importance of Knowsley as a place for the acclimatization of animals was emphasized by Weinland—nine years after the animal collection was sold—in exuberant praise: "For this more recent systematic importation and its splendid results, to be expanded upon below under 'Reproduction' we have occasion to be grateful above all to the English, and among them principally to the Earl of Derby, who has often laid out hundreds of pounds for the acquisition of a breeding pair of antelopes. We can rightly say that his Knowsley menagerie was the first zoological garden and even takes precedence, with respect to the acclimatisation of such animals, which could become truly domesticated, over the old Jardin des Plantes in Paris."[48]

In Weinland, then, one sees an established specialist in zoology elevating Knowsley to an internationally significant place for the acclimatization of animals. In the aforementioned report in *The Gardeners' Chronicle* of August 1841, the importance of Knowsley is also emphasized:

> The principal object of the Earl of Derby, besides a desire to possess living animals for the elucidation of the science of Natural History, has ever been to introduce such animals as are likely to become useful either as food or to furnish materials for manufacturing purposes. His Lordship has been eminently successful as regards the Alpaca or Peruvian sheep, which at the present time occupy so much attention, particularly by those engaged in pastoral pursuits. There is a small flock at Knowsley, and the wool upon them which his Lordship has bred in England is found to be much superior to that imported from South America: . . . . There are

many species of deer, antelopes, and other animals, which his Lordship is attempting to naturalise; but to advert more particularly to the subject would, I fear, occupy more space than the columns of *The Gardeners' Chronicle* would permit. The large collection of pigeons and pheasants adds greatly to the beauty of the aviary. The ostrich, emu, rhea, cassowary, and many other beautiful and rare birds never fail to delight visitors by their grotesque figures and beautiful plumage. There is a numerous collection of carnivorous birds and parrots, both of which engross the visitor's attention. The ponds in the aviary are adorned with a beautiful and valuable collection of rare species of water-fowl from most parts of the world; this assemblage of aquatic birds is said to be the finest in Europe. The Ornithologist would find a rich treat for observation, which would amply repay a visit from any part of the kingdom.[49]

But Knowsley lost its outstanding status in the world of zoology within a very short time. In his later years, the thirteenth Earl apparently devoted his energies increasingly to garden culture, and the animal collection was sold shortly after his death.[50]

The Fourteenth Earl of Derby

The entry in a guidebook published in 1853, *A Visitation of the Seats and Arms of the Noblemen and Gentlemen of Great Britain,* describes Knowsley at the time when Edward George Geoffrey Smith Stanley took over as the fourteenth Earl of Derby:

This splendid demesne is situated in the parish of Huyton, seven miles from Liverpool, and two from Prescot, and is the great ornament to the hundred of West Derby, whence the noble proprietor derives the title of Earl. Knowsley Hall has, perhaps more of the grandeur created by ample dimensions than by architectural style; having been added to and altered according to the taste of various possessors on numerous occasions. . . . The Park of Knowsley is the largest in the county, being between nine and ten miles in circumference. Rich plantations and trees of ancient growth decorate the surface; and a lake of nearly a mile adorns the centre.[51]

The fourteenth Earl of Derby, Edward George Geoffrey Smith Stanley (1799–1869), eldest son of Edward Smith Stanley, was described as "the most brilliant and distinguished of the modern earls."[52] Among other positions, he served three times as prime minister (1852, 1858–59, and 1866–68).[53] Derby was a passionate sportsman and horseman, but he failed during his horse racing career "to win either the Derby or the Oaks, those highlights of the racing calendar established by his grandfather."[54]

He did not share his father's extraordinary interests in zoology and ornithology, and he sold the collection of animals and birds immediately after his father's death in 1851.[55] Apparently, he also disposed of the orchid collection. A few years after the fourteenth Earl had succeeded, an author stated about Knowsley: "The last time I was here there was a good collection of Orchids, and there was also a splendid menagerie. The animals were collected by the late Earl of Derby, and the Orchids also. When the present Earl came into possession they were all disposed of, and the only remains is [sic] an extensive aviary, and a few Orchids in a small stove. The old Orchid-house is converted into a greenhouse filled with well-grown plants, forced Rhododendrons, *Kalmia latifolia*, and many Acacias in bloom."[56]

Nevertheless, Knowsley apparently maintained its standards as a place where horticulture and arboriculture were practiced at a high level. The same author who laments the loss of the collection of orchids introduces his 1855 article on Knowsley with "this is one of what Loudon styles 'first-rate-residences.'"[57] He then praises the "well-trained fruit-trees," the "very good" vines, and, in particular, the excellent cultivation of peaches: "There are three Peach-houses, and the trees were all in fruit in three successions. . . . To produce such a succession there must have been great care and skill bestowed. Forcing is one of the triumphs of gardening art, and in no place is it better exhibited than at Knowsley."[58] An 1865 article on Knowsley proclaims that the Earl "has done something, in his own right, for the advancement of gardening."[59]

The Fifteenth Earl of Derby

Between 1834 and 1869, under the thirteenth and fourteenth Earls of Derby, Knowsley probably developed—in terms of its park, gardens, and horticultural enterprises—into the place Hans Jancke saw when he arrived there in 1874. It is unlikely that the fifteenth Earl of Derby, Edward Henry Stanley (1826–93), the politician and diarist[60] who succeeded his father in 1869, had considerable influence on the parks and gardens of Knowsley, given that his incumbency would have been only of five years at the time of Jancke's visit. As a young man, Edward Henry Stanley visited the West Indies, served briefly as colonial secretary in the 1858–59 government, and rose to the rank of the first secretary of state for India. From July 1866 to December 1868, he was foreign secretary. He was elevated to the lords in February 1870, and from December 1882 on served again as colonial secretary.[61]

An article on Knowsley in *The Gardeners' Chronicle* from 1869 can perhaps elucidate the situation that Jancke might have found there five years later:

Those who may have visited Knowsley four or five years ago, would not have been much struck with its grandeur or extent from a horticultural point of view. The fine Peach and Pear walls, and also the extensive kitchen garden, may have excited admiration, but the structures for the cultivation of fruits and flowers under glass were quite inadequate, and belonged more to the primitive periods of horticulture than to the present day. Now, a very different state of things is seen. The liberality and taste of the noble Earl, and the energy and talent displayed by Mr. Freeman, have completely altered, and that in a very short period of time, the general character of the gardens and fruit-houses, which are teeming with almost every choice variety of fruit in cultivation. Most of the old structures have been cleared away and are replaced by new houses, adapted to the improved system of horticulture.[62]

It was particularly "the cultivation of fruits and flowers under glass" (and fruit cultivation, in general) that fascinated Jancke and that is dealt with in the travel report.

Knowsley and Its Head Gardeners: 1830s to 1870s

To what extent were the parks, gardens, and horticulture at places like Knowsley influenced by their owners or their head gardeners? Brent Elliott has elaborated on the role of the head gardeners, who were responsible for the parks and gardens as well as such horticultural issues as the kitchen garden and the cultivation of orchids, exotic and indigenous plants, and fruit trees: "As far as the ornamental garden was concerned, the gardener's principal duty was simple maintenance. Any scope he had for innovation and attainment of prestige lay in the kitchen garden; and those who did earn fame did so largely for their advances in fruit cultivation, like John Rose, credited with growing the first English pineapple, and William Speechly of Welbeck Abbey, author of a major book on grape cultivation."[63]

The role of the head gardeners at Knowsley in the period under discussion is also reflected in the contemporary horticultural literature. Richard Keyte Yarnall (1725–1826) was head gardener at Knowsley for almost thirty years until his death in 1826. After working as a gardener at Coombe Abbey, Warwickshire, he "went as a journeyman to Hampton Court Gardens, at that time under the celebrated Landscape Gardener, Mr. Brown;"[64] this position was followed by employments with the Earl of Waldegrave at Navestock in Essex and the Earl of Shrewsbury at Heythorpe. In May 1796, he became gardener to the Earl of Derby. In Yarnall's obituary in *The Gardener's Magazine,* little is said about his achievements as head gardener at Knowsley, only that "he gave the highest satisfaction" as a gardener. Apparently, it was more important in this obituary to emphasize that "his noble mistress and master" showed the greatest humanity and kindness to him "in his last illness . . . who rather than hurt the worthy man's feelings by superannuating him, or appointing his successor during his life-time, chose to submit to various privations, and irregularities of management, the inevitable consequence of the want of an active superintendant [*sic*]."[65]

Yarnall's successor was apparently a Mr. Smith. In his "General Results of a Gardening Tour" (1831), J. C. Loudon described the considerable improvements in the quality of the kitchen gardens of Knowsley since his last visit in 1819, when Yarnall was still head gardener: "The kitchen-gardens at Knowlsley [*sic*] Park have been reformed by Mr. Smith, and most admirable crops of grapes, pines, and peaches are now in full perfection. Considering the state that these gardens were in when I saw them in 1819, the greatest credit is due to Mr. Smith."[66]

A report on Knowsley from 1855 states that "Mr. Jenning has been the head-gardener for nearly twenty years."[67] An 1858 article on "Peach Trees and Other Objects at Knowsley" names Jennings "the able and worthy gardener at Knowsley," and comments on the "affluence, good management, and dignity, with which everything is carried out."[68]

In the *Gardeners' Chronicle and Agricultural Gazette* (1869), the considerable improvements that had been made to the gardens during the previous years are described and Freeman is praised as the one responsible for them.[69] Freeman eventually had to resign the superintendence of the gardens because of his failing health.[70] He was succeeded by Harrison, who was the head gardener during Jancke's stay. A note in *The Gardeners' Chronicle* states: "Mr. Harrison is one of the most intelligent and best practical gardeners in England, as the gardens at Osmaston bear witness, his knowledge not being confined to the forcing of fruits and the production of vegetables, but extending to all classes of plants, hardy and exotic."[71] Similarly, the November 1872 issue of *The Garden* heralded Harrison's appointment as head gardener at Knowsley.[72]

A longer quotation from an article published in 1874 may shed light on the state of Knowsley when Hans Jancke arrived. Its author points out that the gardens and the management of the horticultural enterprises had suffered in recent years due to the declining health of the "late gardener" but maintains that Knowsley would soon reestablish under the management of Harrison "the prominent position it [had] always held as a fruit garden":

> Those who approach Knowsley, as I did, from the Liverpool side, fail to see it in its best aspect, for the grand entrance is on the other side, close to the town of Prescot, where stand two lodges with handsome iron gates, and where, as elsewhere throughout the park, the motto of the Stanleys, 'Sans changer,' meets the eye. The park is seven miles in circumference, beautifully wooded, but, to my mind, lacking those grand features which distinguish some I know. This arises in a great measure from the flatness

of the district; and the extent of trees of course in such a case shuts out the view. The house is a large and not very handsome building of various periods, but is said to be comfortable and roomy. . . .

At the period of my visit his lordship's able gardener, Mr. Harrison, was absent, but his very excellent foreman took me through the houses and gardens. One too often hears on going over gardens depreciatory remarks on the last incumbent's work, to be used as a sort of foil to set off the present state of things; but at Knowsley there has been really such a condition. The late gardener was for a very long time in a very bad state of health, and consequently things fell into a very indifferent state. He was at last obliged to resign his post, and has been succeeded by Mr. Harrison, who was lately gardener to Mr. Wright at Osmaston Manor, and under his able management Knowsley will soon reestablish the prominent position it has always held as a fruit garden. There is but little ornamental gardening.[73]

Hans Jancke in Knowsley

The question of why Hans Jancke went to Knowsley has been answered by Brent Elliott in the following way:

At that time it was apparent that the gardens were being restored after a period of comparative neglect; the previous head gardener had finally resigned in 1872 after some years of illness which prevented him from managing the gardens as well as formerly. The new head gardener was Mr Harrison, previously head gardener at Osmaston Manor in Derbyshire; the 1874 article cited above makes it clear that he was in the process of reinvigorating the gardens, but still had a long way to go. All this makes it more puzzling why Jancke should have chosen Knowsley as the place to visit. But Knowsley did have a reputation, based largely on the achievements of the 13th Earl of Derby, who had died in 1851; he had been an enthusiast for botany and natural history generally, and built up a most impressive library, continued by his son (who among other things acquired some of the drawings of Chinese plants which John Reeves had sent from China to the Horticultural Society, and which were sold by the Society in 1859). In the gardens, the 13th Earl had built up a large and important collection of orchids. When Edward Stanley became the 14th Earl, he sold off much of his predecessor's orchid collection (along with most of the exotic livestock) and reduced the burden of garden administration. So it is possible that Knowsley had a lingering reputation for horticultural excellence that might have motivated Jancke to choose it; or maybe the news that the garden was under new management and beginning to return to its former glories had reached Germany.[74]

In all likelihood, the long tradition of and the excellence in the cultivation of fruit, fruit trees, orchids, and other ornamental plants in Knowsley drove Hans Jancke to stay there for one year. In the mid-nineteenth century, Knowsley apparently enjoyed an esteemed horticultural reputation for being a center of fruit cultivation and of exotic plant and hothouse culture; such renown probably drew Jancke to the estate and explains why he devoted his attention almost exclusively to these aspects of it in his report. It may be assumed that his patron, the Königliche Gärtnerlehranstalt Wildpark-Potsdam, sent him there. Hofgartendirektor Ferdinand Jühlke (1815–93), Peter Joseph Lenné's successor as head of the Königliche Gärtnerlehranstalt, was a specialist in fruit and vegetable cultivation, less so in the garden arts; perhaps it was he who sent Jancke—pursuing his own interests—to Knowsley. Under Jühlke's predecessor, Lenné, such a study trip would rather have taken the beneficiary to celebrated shrines of the garden arts.[75] In the introduction to his report, Jancke himself refers to "the good offices of Königlicher Obergärtner Herr *Fintelmann*" through which he received "employment at the *Knowsley Gardens* in the charge of *Mr. Harrison*."[76] Fintelmann, too, could thus have exerted a strong influence on the choice of Jancke's destination.

Hans Jancke drew up his report about his stay in Knowsley at Sanssouci in June 1875.[77] Although the exact dates of his journey are not currently known, he was certainly staying at Knowsley in the summer of 1874 and remained there until 1875.[78] In February 1874, he was notified of the grant from Königliche Gärtnerlehranstalt Wildpark-Potsdam for his journey to England, as recorded in the introduction to his report:

> After I had returned from the field to complete my studies at the Königliche Gärtner-Lehranstalt that had been interrupted by the war with France, Herr Garten-Inspector *Gärdt* graciously granted me a position in the nursery of Herr *Borsig* under his direction, where I worked for one year in the orchid- and hothouses. In the spring of 1873 I went thenceforth to Metz, there to work at the tree nursery of *Simon Louis Frères*, and found employment in the autumn of that same year at *Linden's* establishment near Ghent. Here I was delighted to receive, in February of 1874, news of a beneficent grant of 100 Thaler from the Königliche Gärtner-Lehranstalt for a study journey to England, conjoined with the injunction to compile a report of my experiences upon my return. Through the good offices of Königlicher Obergärtner Herr *Fintelmann* I was invited to take up employment at the *Knowsley Gardens* in the charge of *Mr. Harrison*, a property of the *Earl of Derby*, where I found ample opportunity to

broaden my knowledge, whereof in the following, according to my commission, I humbly allow myself to give a closer account.[79]

Several pages of English-language exercises found among the Jancke papers in the archives of the Stiftung Preußische Schlösser und Gärten Berlin-Brandenburg suggest that he prepared diligently for his journey to Knowsley. He also ascribed importance to compiling comprehensive reports on his journeys connected with his work and to the significant stages of his professional life; he wrote, for example, a report "über das Lindensche Etablissement zu Gent," where he had apparently stayed from autumn 1873 to spring 1874.[80] He also compiled a report on a fact-finding trip to Lower Saxony in 1904.[81]

Notes on Hans Jancke's Travel Journal

Of exceptional significance, however, is the extensive and detailed notes on his stay of almost a year at Knowsley in 1874–75. The value that he attached to the compilation of this report may be inferred from a ninety-nine-page manuscript—found among the Hans Oskar Jancke Papers in the Stiftung Preußische Schlösser und Gärten archives—which probably served as a draft for the final version.[82]

Jancke's report is devoted almost exclusively to the cultivation of fruit, vegetables, and ornamental plants at Knowsley as well as the technical aspects of greenhouse construction; his remarks on its gardens and park,[83] their design and garden aesthetic aspects, take up only a few pages. This is all the more astonishing because he was dealing with a thoroughly noteworthy example of the garden arts—a subject in which he was well educated and interested. His competence was demonstrated, for instance, in 1882, when he was commissioned by Jühlke to draw up a modernization plan for Schlosspark Bellevue (Figure 7). It was to be "splendid, orderly and colourful. The filling-in of the park's lakes, planned in 1880, was carried out at the behest of the Crown Princess or at least begun. Jancke's plan may well have been a factor in his succeeding Kühne as Hofgärtner in Bellevue in 1884."[84]

Jancke's firm interest in the design of gardens and parks may also be inferred from the fact that he surveyed and drew a map of the gardens (at least, the "inner garden") (see Plate 13) at the beginning of his stay at Knowsley.[85] On the park itself, Jancke's report expends few words, offering the following description in the first few pages:

The _Knowsley Gardens_ lie in the finest part of the rainy county of _Lancashire,_ in the midst of flourishing villages and extensive woodland. The terrain is of gently rolling hills, gradually undulating downward from north-northeast to south-southwest. Beautiful ancient trees, mostly _Acer,_

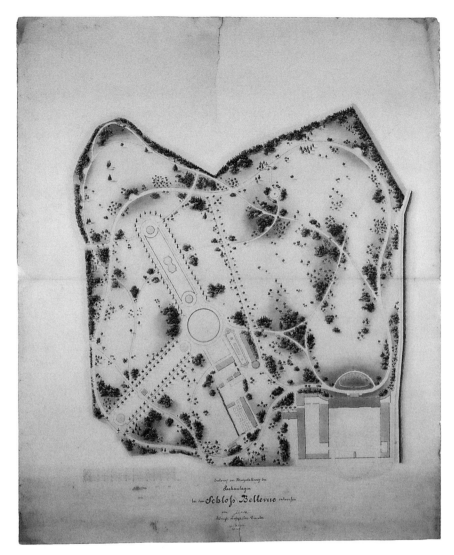

figure 7

Sketch for the new design of the park at the Bellevue Palace.

Hans Oskar Jancke papers, Stiftung Preußische Schlösser und Gärten Berlin-Brandenburg (SPSG), F0019306. (Photograph: Daniel Lindner)

Aesculus, Castanea, Fagus, Quercus, Tilia & Ulmus tower above the dense underbrush, which to the greatest extent consists of evergreen shrubs: *Ilex, Buxus, Cupressus, Thuja, Taxus,* and masses of *Rhododendron,* surrounding the kitchen-, fruit-, and flower garden, the fruit forcing houses, stalls, etc., while more recent plantings of trees and shrubs, some evergreen, some deciduous, pleasantly punctuate the well-tended, perpetually lush green lawns surrounding the castle. The maritime climate with its mild winters makes it possible for a few specimens of *Araucaria imbricata* and *Cedrus Deodara* to thrive, while the cool summers do not promote the growth of trees with pinnate leaves and they are sparsely represented; *Robinia, Gleditschia*, and the like are completely absent. A few other trees, very common in our land, such as *Betula, Fraxinus,* and *Platanus* make a very weak showing here. . . . For a closer understanding of the same [the plan of the inner park] I permit myself the following explanatory remarks:

The *Knowsley Gardens* are completely separated from the adjacent *Knowsley Park* by iron railings, their main purpose being to prevent the incursions of the numerous red and fallow deer. The *Gardens* are bordered on two sides by lakes (A, B, C & D on the plan), notable less for their fine forms as for their extraordinarily clear, clean water and enormous stocks of fish. The houses and lakes adjoining the *Gardens* are enclosed with masonry walls, bearing a part of the railings.

Lake A, bordering the garden to the east, is around six hundred meters long and 250 meters wide. On the opposite shore a range of low hills rise, which in summer is covered with head-high bracken (*Pteris aquilina*) that fructifies abundantly every year; from this ground there rise numerous ancient coniferous and deciduous trees, overlooked by an old ruined tower. The lake offers a wonderful view from the fisherman's cottage r, in which splendid boats for pleasure trips in summer are kept. Lake A lies higher than the greater part of the garden and supplies the same by means of a many-branched system of pipes with clear, potable water. The paths that run along its shore are but a few meters above its surface. The water level of Lake B lies about sixteen meters lower than that of A, that of C yet another 1.5 meters lower than B, and the water level of D lies some four meters lower than that of C; unfortunately I lacked the time for a more precise measurement of the height differences, which I would dearly like to have made. The aforementioned lakes are connected with each other and with the four smaller ponds in the middle of the garden by robust underground pipes with stopcocks, by means of which sudden rises in the water levels in spring and already at the end of winter are controlled. Lake D has an outflow at its western end to the lakes in the outer park. As yet there are no fountains, although they could have been built quite easily and at no great expense but, as *Mr. Harrison* intimated to me, it is intended to erect a fountain in the next few years in place of the large Rhododendron bush, located at the center of the extensive flower parterre to the east of the castle. With regard to the plantings in the parterre, of the eight s-shaped beds four are usually planted with a centerline of *Achyranthes Verschaffetli* and a surround of *Pyrethrum Parthenium var. aureum*, the other four with *Iresine Lindeni* and *Gnaphalium tomentosum* as surround. The remaining beds are planted with Scarlet Pelargoniums.[86]

Hans Jancke offers not a romantic depiction of a glorious landscape park and its integration in the surrounding countryside but rather a dry, technically inclined presentation that highlights details such as Lake B lay sixteen meters lower than Lake A, and Lake C another one and a half meters lower than Lake B, and so on. He digresses from a planned fountain to the planting-out of the parterre. And from the ninth page of this extensive and detailed report, he concerns himself mainly with Knowsley as a place for the production of plants; the cultivation of indigenous and foreign fruit trees, shrubs, and ornamental plants; and the propagation of these plants in the greenhouses and forcing houses.[87] Jancke devotes special attention in this connection to the construction of the Knowsley greenhouses and the technology applied within them. He found some of the greenhouses so remarkable that he executed detailed drawings of them: "Many of the houses, namely the newer ones, are constructed in exemplary fashion, and I have therefore executed precise drawings of some of them, which I include in the single chapters on the forcing of diverse species of fruit."[88] His technical bent found expression in numerous detailed drawings depicting some of the greenhouses in plan and cross section.

In what follows, it cannot be our concern to evaluate the quality, diversity, and peculiarities of the plants cultivated at Knowsley, as may be gathered from Jancke's report; we can only make a few observations and raise questions for future research. It could be of interest to investigate whether Jancke applied his newfound knowledge on greenhouse construction or the cultivation of ornamental plants, fruit trees, and shrubs upon his return to Germany (for example, at Bellevue).

With the exception of Mr. Harrison, the report manages to get by with hardly a reference to the gardening colleagues with whom Jancke became acquainted at Knowsley.[89] In contrast, Jancke took great care to comprehensively list individual species and varieties, beginning with plants in the ornamental beds and the parterre, as this remark from the report attests: "To the north of the parterre described above lies the _Conservatory_, consisting of a hot and a camellia section and connected to the castle by a corridor. In each section there is a central bed and two side beds in which some very fine and valuable plants stand. Among the plants to be found in the hothouse section one may mention as worthy of recommendation: four very vigorous specimens of _Musa Cavendishi_, which bear fruit annually, two large specimens of _Cycas revoluta_, and additionally . . . ."[90]

This is followed by a list of more than thirty-five species and varieties, among them _Bambusa gracilis_ [_Drepanostachyum falcatum_], _Strelitzia ovata_, and _Passiflora quadrangularis_; the latter was also given special mention in the entry on "Orangery" by G. W. Johnson in _A Dictionary of Modern Gardening_ (1847) as being particularly remarkable.[91] When Jancke mentions that he fertilized a few blooms of _Passiflora edulis_ with pollen from _Passiflora quadrangularis_, all of which then bore fruit "which unfortunately had not quite ripened before [his] departure,"[92] we can presume that they were intended for Potsdam and/or Berlin. Jancke devoted particular attention in a comprehensive chapter on the kitchen garden to the north of the castle and its "well-tended fruit plantings, greenhouses and forcing houses, hotbeds, etc. . . ."[93]

Among the trees at the south-facing walls of the Kitchen Garden are peach, apricot, and pear trees. "The former are entirely trained in fans, with the following varieties: *Noblesse*, early fruiting and very suitable for forcing, *Royal George*, also much used for forcing, *Bellegarde*, equally worthy of recommendation, well suited for transportation as it keeps longer after picking than the other varieties."[94]

Pears seemed to have been, among other fruits, a speciality of the head gardeners at Knowsley. *The Gardeners' Chronicle* (1886) states: "Hardy fruits, in common with other things grown at Knowsley, are thoroughly well done. There is a large extent of wall covered with various kinds of fruit trees in beautiful condition which bear well. Of Apricots there is a full crop set, with Peaches and Nectarines equally plentiful. An extensive collection of Pears is grown, most of the best varieties, bearing well, not only on the walls, but in the shape of large bushes and pyramids, which occupy the sides of the walk; the same remarks apply to Apples, which, with the Pears, are models of skillful management."[95] Jancke lists numerous varieties of pear, and he remarks on some of them with precise observations (as with other fruits), for example: "The <u>Pears</u> cultivated against the south walls are, in the order in which they ripen, as follows: *Williams's bon chrétien*, provides great quantities of delicious fruit in August already, *British Queen*, September, *Duchesse d'Angoulême*, bore only a few fruit in the previous year at *Knowsley* and would only, I was told, provide a good yield in exceptionally warm years, *Gansels Bergamot*, bore no good fruit, *Marie Louise* is only bettered in its copious yield by *Glout Morceau*, while they are probably equal in the goodness of their fruit."[96]

Elucidations of specific ways of cultivation—such as training in pyramid, fan, and oblique palmette forms—also abound: "Against the walls a few single trees were trained in fan shape and in oblique palmette form; all the rest were trained in horizontal palmettes. The pear trees in pyramid form are located in the narrow beds on either side of the Kitchen Garden paths, alternating with apple trees."[97]

Also noteworthy is that Jancke very seldom draws comparisons between the gardening routines and peculiarities found in Knowsley and the practices and state of gardening in Germany, such as in Berlin and Potsdam, or other countries. One exception is when he casts an eye toward fruit growing in Belgium and France: "Although the yield from the *Knowsley* pear trees cannot compare with that achieved in Belgium, France and Lorraine, the reason is probably to be found solely in the moist climate and the less warm summers, and the harvest is still such that one could regard the means employed and the trouble taken as receiving its reward."[98]

After listing and commenting on the varieties of apple grown at Knowsley—almost thirty in number[99]—as well as the plums and cherries, the author finally comes to write on one of the principal topics of his stay: the greenhouses, both unheated and heated forcing houses with the heating technology and techniques employed there. He leads the reader there ("Proceeding now to the plant and forcing houses"), and then lists twenty-five houses, starting with ten grapevine houses, continuing with peach, melon, pineapple, and other houses, and ending with a fig house, all of them "heated by a <u>hot-water system</u> . . . ."[100] He then comments once again on the plants grown in each house with reference to their particularities and qualities. House No. 18 would contain plants from the East Indies and the South Sea Islands, among them *Aerides Fieldingii, Phalaenopsis amabilis,* and *Anthurium leuconeurum.*[101] Innumerable other species follow. For House No. 19 alone, Jancke's catalogue extends over more than six pages of "the following notable plants,"[102] among them *Ada aurantiaca, Calanthe Masuca,* and *Cattleya labiata* to *Aralia leptophylla* and *Gardenia citriodora (Mitriostigma axillare).*[103]

Viniculture at Knowsley as part of fruit cultivation is also accorded great attention. Jancke emphasizes the quality of the grapes, remarking that "the grapes grown there not only equal but even surpass in size, coloration, and taste those of lands whose climate is far more propitious for viniculture" and that "one . . . has a supply of ripe grapes the whole year round."[104] His praise of the quality of viniculture in the Knowsley gardens is confirmed by contemporary reports in horticultural magazines. An 1858 article on "Peach Trees and Other Objects at Knowsley" relates that "the Vines looked remarkably well, and bore excellent crops of well-coloured fruit, which would have run some of the crack Show men a hard race, at some of the Metropolitan meetings, if they had been exhibited there; but Mr. Jennings, the able and worthy gardener at Knowsley, does not send to these Shows."[105] Almost three decades later, the horticultural press still emphasized the superiority of viniculture at Knowsley: "There are nine vineries, most of which run from 60 to some 80 feet long, and wide in proportion; the Vines collectively are in fine order, carrying excellent crops."[106]

In connection with the excellent viniculture, Jancke makes one of his infrequent comparisons to the situation in other countries: "In the year 1874 all the houses yielded a very rich harvest of large and well-formed grapes the like of which I have not yet seen on the Continent. No less plentiful results were achieved in the <u>peach forcing</u>."[107] This quality was presumably why he directed his graphic attentions particularly to the greenhouses used for viniculture.[108] He explains some of the houses in great detail—the construction, the technology used, the soil culture, and the fertilization methods.[109] Differentiated descriptions of the Knowsley viniculture methods are also included: "Shortly before sprouting begins the soil is covered as far as the roots extend with a six-centimeter-thick layer of fresh cow or pig manure. In each successive year the old manure is removed and replaced with fresh. If, after several years, the soil is exhausted or some vines have rotten roots, the soil is partially replaced, which happens in the following manner."[110]

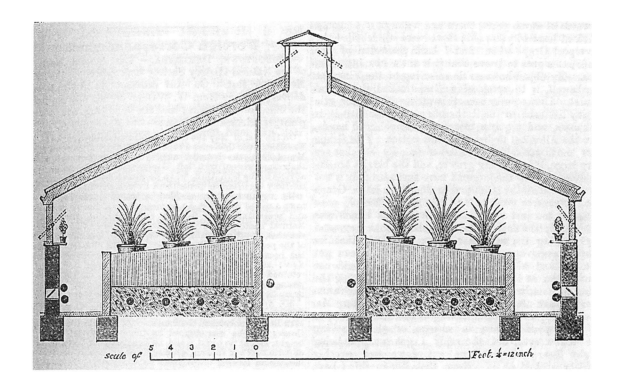

scale of   5 4 3 2 1 0   ]Feet. ¼=12inch

figure 8
House for the
cultivation of
pineapple in
Knowsley, from *The
Gardeners' Chronicle
and Agricultural
Gazette* (February 11,
1865): 125.

It seems only natural that, considering the notice Jancke paid to the cultivation of grapes and other sensitive produce, he also directed his attention to pests and their control in his report.[111] Of the various methods he describes, one example will serve: "Mice are very fond of Muscat grapes, and therefore one places a piece of matting over each bunch with the rough side up. The mice do not like to touch the matting with their feet and the grapes remain untouched."[112]

Along with viniculture, the growing of pineapples seems to have been important at Knowsley, and Jancke allots several pages of his report to them. In the case of the pineapples, it seems that the "ordinary" cow or pig manure was not used but that the pineapple plants were watered with "liquid manure (prepared from deer dung)."[113] Jancke's emphasis on the pineapples in Knowsley is convincingly confirmed by numerous articles in contemporary horticultural journals,[114] among them one that is dedicated explicitly to "The Pine Stove at Knowsley": "Greatly indeed was the writer pleased to find that Knowsley represents gardening so well, and that in this fine old establishment there is accommodation for the cultivation of the king of fruits of a kind which must command universal admiration. All ye cultivators of the Pine-apple [...] listen while I describe the quantity and quality of the fruit."[115] The author then describes the house (Figure 8) for the cultivation of the fruit, one hundred feet long and twenty-six feet wide, "containing as near as may be 600 plants .... This much I may say, that if ever there was a model house for the cultivation of the Pine, certainly this is the house. The principle is good, and worthy of adoption; the size and details can be modified according to circumstances. Any lady fastidious about her person and dress can walk through, inspect, and admire this house quite unconcernedly, so different is it from an older style of house, where the narrow passages and whitewashed walls are always a serious obstruction to capacious skirts."[116] It remains unclear whether Jancke had referred to the same house that was described in *The Gardeners' Chronicle* a decade earlier.

In 1890, a writer commented on the Pine house in the Knowsley garden, as "a matter to be mentioned in these days of imported fruits, when the growth of Pines at many great establishments has been abandoned."[117]

The cultivation of melons[118] and strawberries[119] is described by Jancke in cursory fashion. In connection with vegetable growing, one finds probably the very first direct comparison to German methods: "<u>Vegetable growing</u> at *Knowsley* is in general the same as here.... <u>Mushroom growing</u> does not differ from ours at home."[120]

That Jancke's interest was directed almost entirely toward the cultivation of individual plants and not to the garden arts may also be inferred from the description of a visit to Kew Gardens, which concluded his stay of almost a year; after leaving Knowsley, he paid these grounds a visit on his way back to Germany—but there, too, it seems that only the plants, not the park and its design, were of any interest:

> On my return journey from England to Germany I stayed, as on the outward journey, in London for a few days in order to visit the famous *Kew Gardens* with the splendid, extensive museums, the beautiful great Palm House, the incomparable fern collection, etc., and also to visit the large establishments of *Veitch, Bull, Williams,* and *Henderson* again.
> Unfortunately my time was too short to look around the aforementioned establishments and the botanic garden with its rich plant treasures as fully as I would have liked. Nevertheless I had numerous opportunities to make highly interesting notes about plant care and cultivation, the propagation and distribution of useful plants (in the *Kew Museum*), etc., and to see cultivated plants of all species in an extraordinary perfection, along with many large and fine examples of <u>novelties</u>, of which to conclude I wish to mention a few:
> *Allocasia Marshalli*
> [*Allocasia*] *illustris,* both are similar to *A. Jenningsii* but *A. Marshalli* has markedly larger leaves, while *illustris* differs from *A. Jenningsii* in a silver-gray patch in the center of the leaf. Of *Anthurium Scherzerianum album* I saw a very striking example at *William's,* which however was not blooming when I was there.[121]

After three more pages listing the species and varieties of plants found at Kew Gardens, Jancke's report ends on page 122. This implies that the beauties of park grounds and the ideas and theories underlying their aesthetics and design were, in Jancke's view, not particularly "newsworthy"; his interest was in horticulture and arboriculture, in the diversity of plants and their propagation, in greenhouse technology—these interests and scientific curiosities are impressively documented in his report. Many questions remain: Why was Knowsley the chosen destination for his study journey? Was it his personal interest? Or had his patron, the Königliche Gärtnerlehranstalt, sent him there? If so, with what motives? Did the impulse come from Ferdinand Jühlke? Or from the Königlicher Oberhofgärtner Fintelmann, whom Jancke mentions in the introduction to his report as the one who secured him a place at Knowsley? The quality of the plants kept at Knowsley in the 1870s, the apparently enormous diversity of fruit trees and shrubs, and the multifarious exotic decorative plants would also be an interesting topic in comparison with the situation on other estates of the time.

To me, of particular interest is the question of whether, on his return to Germany (and particularly at Bellevue), Jancke applied the knowledge and ideas he had collected at Knowsley to his own horticulture and garden art. Another worthy inquiry would be into whether Jancke brought his own specific knowledge of plant propagation and the cultivation of fruit trees, shrubs, and exotic decorative plants to Knowsley, knowledge that perhaps found applications there—whether, that is, he could "fertilize" the Knowsley gardening culture. To those who wish to pursue the concomitant questions; to research specialists in garden history, horticulture, and the garden arts; and also to practitioners of garden heritage conservation, I hope that this volume, with its transcription of Hans Jancke's report, will provide valuable impetus and assistance.

Notes to the Introduction

1 See, for example, Gabriele M. Knoll, *Kulturgeschichte des Reisens: Von der Pilgerfahrt zum Badeurlaub* (Darmstadt: Wissenschaftliche Buchgesellschaft, 2006); and Attilio Brilli, *Als Reisen eine Kunst war: Vom Beginn des modernen Tourismus; Die "Grand Tour"* (Berlin: Wagenbach, 2001).

2 See, for example, Marcus Köhler, *Frühe Landschaftsgärten in Rußland und Deutschland: Johann Busch als Mentor eines neuen Stils* (Berlin: Aland-Verlag, 2003), particularly the chapter "Deutsche Adlige auf Englandreise," 70ff.; see also Marcus Köhler, "Gärten, Äcker und Fabriken—Englandreisen hannoverscher Adliger im ausgehenden 18. Jahrhundert," in *Reisen in Parks und Gärten: Umrisse einer Rezeptions—und Imaginationsgeschichte*, ed. Hubertus Fischer, Sigrid Thielking, and Joachim Wolschke-Bulmahn (Munich: Martin Meidenbauer, 2012).

3 See the references to time spent abroad by numerous professional gardeners from Germany during the late nineteenth and early twentieth centuries in Gert Gröning and Joachim Wolschke-Bulmahn, *Grüne Biographien: Biographisches Handbuch zur Landschaftsarchitektur in Deutschland im frühen 20. Jahrhundert* (Berlin and Hannover: Patzer Verlag, 1997).

4 Cf. Michael Seiler and Clemens Wimmer, "Wie Hofgärtner reisten," in *Preußisch Grün: Hofgärtner in Brandenburg-Preußen* (Potsdam: Henschel Verlag, 2004), 169.

5 Gröning and Wolschke-Bulmahn, *Grüne Biographien*, 51 (#249).

6 Ibid., 58 (#295).

7 Ibid., 138 (#858).

8 Ibid., 219 (#1407).

9 Ibid., 220 (#1413).

10 Ibid., 257 (#1606).

11 Seiler and Wimmer, "Wie Hofgärtner reisten," 172. For Austrian court gardeners, see Jochen Martz, "In kaiserlicher Mission unterwegs in 'berühmten Gärten fremder Länder'—Reiseberichte österreichischer Hofgärtner des 19. Jahrhunderts," in *Reisen in Parks und Gärten: Umrisse einer Rezeptions—und Imaginationsgeschichte*, ed. Hubertus Fischer, Sigrid Thielking, and Joachim Wolschke-Bulmahn (Munich: Martin Meidenbauer, 2012), 427–46.

12 Clemens Wimmer, "Zwischen Hofhandwerk und Zunft. Zur sozialen Stellung der Hofgärtner," in *Preußisch Grün: Hofgärtner in Brandenburg-Preußen* (Potsdam: Henschel Verlag, 2004), 128f.

13 Seiler and Wimmer, "Wie Hofgärtner reisten," 172.

14 Ibid., 172.

15 Theodor Echtermeyer, ed., *Führer durch die Königliche Gärtnerlehranstalt Dahlem (bei Berlin-Steglitz)* (Berlin: Parey, 1913).

16 Such as the Königlicher Kronenorden 4. Klasse, Kriegsdenkmünze 1870/71, Landwehrdienstauszeichnung, Erinnerungsmedaille 1897, Ritterkreuz 2. Klasse des Großherzoglichen Badischen Ordens vom Zähringer Löwen, den Persischen Sonnen- und Löwenorden, den Königlichen Roten Adlerorden 4. Klasse, das Erinnerungszeichen zur Silbernen Hochzeit

Ihrer Majestäten, 1906, and the Vermeilmedaille of the Deutsche Gartenbaugesellschaft 1913 (cf. Echtermeyer, *Führer durch die Königliche Gärtnerlehranstalt Dahlem*, 194).

17 Cf. *Preußisch Grün*, 230; on the social standing of royal gardeners, see Clemens Alexander Wimmer, *Die preußischen Hofgärtner* (Berlin: Druckhaus Hentrich, 1996), 22–27.

18 *Die Gartenwelt* 24 (1920): 76.

19 See, for example, William Page, ed., *The Victoria History of the Counties of England: A History of the County of Lancashire,* vol. 3 (1907; repr., Brussels: Jos. Adams, 1966), 157–68.

20 Entry on "Knowsley Park" in the conference brochure for the Garden Historical Society, Annual General Meeting and Summer Conference, Liverpool, July 3–6, 2008.

21 In Thomas Hinde, *Capability Brown: The Story of a Master Gardener* (London: Hutchinson, 1986), there is no reference to Knowsley; in Dorothy Stroud, *Capability Brown* (1950; repr., London and Boston: Faber and Faber, 1984), one finds only a reference to "Knowsley, Lancs." with the "House and Map Number" 113, the client, "The Earl of Derby Order of Lord Strange," and under notes: "Plans given for 'alterations' and £100 received on account in 1775. Further plans supplied for the kitchen garden and 'grounds round the house' now much changed," 231.

22 In an e-mail of August 28, 2012, Brent Elliott wrote: "Dorothy Stroud's reference to Knowsley is based on the entry in Brown's account book, which we hold in the RHS Library. That is really the primary piece of evidence for Brown's involvement by the time the gardening press got going in the 1820s."

23 I would like to thank Ms. Kirstin Waibel, curator of collections, The Derby Collection Image Library, Knowsley, for making available a reproduction of this publication (License granted courtesy of The Rt. Hon. The Earl of Derby, 2009).

24 Anna Sholl, *The Historical Development of Knowsley Park: A Study of the Landscape, 1085–1985* (Published for the Groundwork Trust, 1985), 19; license granted courtesy of The Rt. Hon. The Earl of Derby, 2009.

25 See on this, for example, the chapter "The Victorian Period, 1830–1900," in ibid., 27–29.

26 H. C. G. Matthew and Brian Harrison, eds., *Oxford Dictionary of National Biography: From the Earliest Time to the Year 2000,* vol. 52 (Oxford: Oxford University Press, 2004), 203–4.

27 Ibid., 204.

28 Ibid., 204. On the significance of the thirteenth Earl of Derby in the field of natural history and zoology, see Clemency Fisher and Christine E. Jackson, "The 13th Earl of Derby as a Scientist," in *A Passion for Natural History: The Life and Legacy of the 13th Earl of Derby,* ed. Clemency Fisher (Liverpool: The Bluecoat Press, 2002), 50.

29 Unnamed correspondent, "Knowsley Hall—the Seat of the Earl of Derby," *The Gardeners' Chronicle* (August 28, 1841): 567. Similarly, Woolfall points out Derby's interest in species "that he considered would be either ornamental or useful if successfully naturalized," in S. J. Woolfall, "History of the 13th Earl of Derby's Menagerie and Aviary at Knowsley Hall, Liverpool (1806–1851)," *Archives of Natural History* 17 (1990): 1, 8.

30 Ibid., 567.

31 Brent Elliott drew my attention to the following articles: *The Gardener's Magazine* 1 (1826): 228–29; *The Gardener's Magazine* 7 (1831): 550; *The Gardeners' Chronicle* (August 28, 1841): 567; *The Cottage Gardener* (April 6, 1858): 1–2; *The Gardeners' Chronicle* (February 11, 1865): 124–25; *The Gardeners' Chronicle and Agricultural Gazette* (June 12, 1869): 643–44; *The Gardeners' Chronicle* (December 30, 1871): 1682; *The Gardeners' Chronicle* (November 9, 1872): 1486; *The Garden* (November 9, 1872): 398; *Journal of Horticulture and Cottage Gardener* (June 18, 1874): 490–92; and *Journal of Horticulture and Home Farmer* (March 3, 1910): 187–91.

32 "In Hooker's 'Icones Plantarum,' t. 594 (1843) there is a figure of *Burkea africana*, named in compliment to Mr. J. Burke, who accomplished a most extensive journey into the interior of South Africa with the object of collecting plants and animals for the Rt. Hon. The Earl of Derby, and fulfilled his mission in so satisfactory a manner that he is now on the point of embarking on a similar errand for Lord Derby and the Royal Botanic Gardens of Kew conjointly, to visit Hudson's Bay, and then proceed westward across the Rocky Mountains to N.W. America and California, where we trust he will be equally successful as in Africa." J. H. D., "Knowsley Hall. Chief Seat of the Earl of Derby, K. G., Prescot—Lancashire," *Supplement to the Journal of Horticulture and Home Farmer* (March 3, 1910): 188.

33 George William Johnson, *A Dictionary of Modern Gardening* (Philadelphia: Lea and Blanchard, 1847), 404.

34 Ibid., 404. In similar fashion the same dictionary refers to Knowsley in the entry on 'CITRUS.' "The following extracts from an essay by Mr. Jones, gardener at Knowsley, exhibits the successful practice in cultivating this genus, pursued by Mr. Durden, gardener at Hurst House, Lancashire." (Ibid., 151).

35 "Garden Memoranda. Knowsley Hall," *The Gardeners' Chronicle* 11 (August 1841): 567.

36 Alexander Somerville, *The Whistler at the Plough: Containing Travels, Statistics, and Descriptions of Scenery and Agricultural Customs in Most Parts of England; With Letters from Ireland* (Manchester: James Ainsworth, 1852).

37 Ibid., 209f.

38 Somerville, by contrast, made observations on industry, the pollution from industrial manufacturing, the contrast between the railways and factories and the beauty of the rural cultural landscape, and the sometimes pitiful living conditions among the landscape's residents. See, for example, his description in ibid., 208.

39 Nancy P. Ševčenko has discussed this topic with examples from Byzantine garden and landscape culture. See Nancy P. Ševčenko, "Wild Animals in the Byzantine Park" in *Byzantine Garden Culture,* ed. Antony Littlewood, Henry Maguire, and Joachim Wolschke-Bulmahn (Washington, D.C.: Dumbarton Oaks Research Library and Collection, 2002), 69–86.

40 Cf. Sally Festing, "Menageries and the Landscape Garden," *Journal of Garden History* 8, no. 4 (1988): 104–17.

41 Ibid., 108.

42 Ibid., 109.

43 Ibid., 111.

44 Mark Laird, "This Other Eden: The American Connection in Georgian Pleasure Grounds, from Shrubbery and Menagerie to Aviary and Flower Garden," in *Knowing Nature: Art and Science in Philadelphia*, ed. Amy R. W. Meyers (New Haven: Yale University Press, 2011), 97.

45 D. F. Weinland, "Was ein Zoologischer Garten leisten soll," *Der Zoologische Garten* 2, no. 1 (1860): 1–11.

46 Ibid., 3. (All quotations are from the English translation.)

47 Ibid., 4.

48 Ibid., 5. In this connection Weinland also refers the reader to *Gleanings from the Menagerie and Aviary of Knowsley Hall* (Hoofed Quadrupeds, Knowsley, 1850) as an important source on the acclimatization of mammals (cf. ibid., 6). In a list following the article, of mammals that had already bred in captivity, Knowsley is mentioned well over twenty times for such diverse species as alpaca, wapiti, zebra, Virginia deer, American auroch, and Sattel-antelope mentioned for the years 1839–1856 (cf. ibid., 8–11).

49 *The Gardeners' Chronicle* 11 (August 1841): 567.

50 "Lord Derby increasingly turned to horticulture. After his death, at the end of June 1851, the living collections were sold by auction over several days from 6th October" (Clemency Fisher, "The Knowsley Aviary and Menagerie," in *A Passion for Natural History: The Life and Legacy of the 13th Earl of Derby*, ed. Clemency Fisher [Liverpool: The Bluecoat Press, 2002], 93).

51 John Bernard Burke, *A Visitation of the Seats and Arms of the Noblemen and Gentlemen of Great Britain*, vol. 2 (London: Hurst and Blackett, 1853), 113.

52 Page, *Victoria History*, 166.

53 http://www.victorianweb.org/graphics/portraits/derby1a.jpg, accessed November 30, 2009.

54 Matthew and Harrison, *Oxford Dictionary*, 185.

55 Cf. Matthew and Harrison, *Oxford Dictionary*, 179.

56 T. Appleby, "Knowsley Park: The Seat of the Earl of Derby," in *The Cottage Gardener, and Country Gentleman's Companion* 14 (1855): 73.

57 Ibid., 72.

58 Ibid., 73.

59 J. A., "The Pine Stowe at Knowsley," *The Gardeners' Chronicle and Agricultural Gazette* (February 11, 1865): 124.

60 Matthew and Harrison, *Oxford Dictionary*, 191.

61 Regarding these and other professional stations of the fifteenth Earl, see Matthew and Harrison, *Oxford Dictionary*, 191ff.

62 J. Wills, "Knowsley, the Seat of the Right Hon. The Earl of Derby," *The Gardeners' Chronicle and Agricultural Gazette* (June 12, 1869): 643.

63 Brent Elliott, *Victorian Gardens* (London: B. T. Batsford, 1986), 13.

64 "Obituary," *The Gardener's Magazine* 1 (1826): 228.

65 Ibid., 229.

66 J. C. Loudon, "General Results of a Gardening Tour," *The Gardener's Magazine* 7 (1831): 550.

67 Appleby, "Knowsley Park," 72.

68 John Robson, "Peach Trees and Other Objects at Knowsley," *The Cottage Gardener and Country Gentleman's Companion* 20 (April 6, 1858): 2.

69 Wills, "Knowsley," 643.

70 *The Gardeners' Chronicle* (November 9, 1872): 1486.

71 Ibid., 1486.

72 "MR. HARRISON, for the last ten years manager of the beautiful gardens at Osmaston Manor, has been appointed head gardener at Knowsley, the seat of the Earl of Derby. We are pleased to find that such a thorough practical gardener has been appointed to conduct the affairs of so important a garden, and we have every confidence that the general state of cultivation in the above gardens, under his able management, will be second to none in this country" (*The Garden* [November 9, 1872], 398).

73 D., "Knowsley Hall: The Seat of the Right Hon. The Earl of Derby," *Journal of Horticulture and Cottage Gardener* (June 18, 1874): 491.

74 Brent Elliott, e-mail message to author, August 29, 2012.

75 I would like to thank Clemens Alexander Wimmer for pointing this out. See also Wimmer, *Die preußischen Hofgärtner*; on Hofgartendirektor Jühlke, his "field of specialization was completely different from that of Lenné. Instead of the garden arts he was a master of fruit and vegetable growing" (109).

76 Hans Jancke, *Reise-Bericht* (Potsdam, 1875), 2. The handwritten manuscript is in the Rare Book Collection, Dumbarton Oaks Research Library and Collection, RBR D-1-2 JAN.

77 Ibid, 1.

78 He gave an account of the planting up of the "flower parterre" to the east of the palace in summer 1874 (cf. ibid., 9–10).

79 Ibid., 1–2.

80 SPSG, Jancke papers, Schachtel III, Mappe 467, Nr. 12, Linden. "Bericht über das Lindensche Etablissement zu Gent" (handwritten manuscript).

81 SPSG, Jancke papers, Schachtel III, Mappe 468, report of 18.8.1904, "Informationsreise nach Niedersachsen."

82 SPSG, Jancke papers, Schachtel III, Mappe 467, Nr. 14.

83 In his introduction, Jancke distinguished between the two categories "Knowsley Gardens" and "Knowsley Park" (cf. Jancke, *Reise-Bericht*, 6).

84 Wimmer, "Zwischen Hofhandwerk und Zunft," 97.

85 At some point this plan later disappeared from the report, which found its way to Dumbarton Oaks in 1995; Michael Rohde, director of the Stiftung Preußische Schlösser und Gärten, informed me that this plan had been acquired about ten years ago previously with part of the Jancke papers. Jancke described his intentions with the plan: "Soon after my arrival at Knowsley the wish grew in me to possess a plan of the inner park, and when one of my colleagues offered to assist me with the surveying and after acquiring a surveyor's chain and cross-staff—the purchase of a compass or a theodolite, which would have eased the survey greatly, was beyond my means—we set to work and had, during our free time almost every day after work, completed almost half the task we had set ourselves. Then my assistant was hindered from carrying on with our surveying so that I was thrown back upon my own resources. At first I considered it almost impossible to complete the work without help, especially as I also had to use my free time on the one hand to write up my notes on the plant forcing, on the other hand to review what I had learned earlier, but eventually I brought the work to its desired conclusion and was in a position to complete the plan from my draft; I enclose it with my report" (Jancke, *Reise-Bericht*, 4–6.).

86 Ibid., 3–4, 6–10.

87 The term "greenhouse" (in the original, "Gewächshaus") is used to apply to the various types of houses: greenhouse, forcing house, hothouse, cold house, etc.

88 Jancke, *Reise-Bericht*, 43.

89 See the references to Mr. Harrison in the report on pages 2, 9, and 60. Harrison was, according to Jancke's report, the Knowsley Gardens administrator.

90 Ibid., 12–13.

91 Cf. the entry for "orangery" in Johnson, *Dictionary of Modern Gardening*, 404.

92 Jancke, *Reise-Bericht*, 13–14.

93 Ibid., 17.

94 Ibid., 17–18.

95 "Knowsley Hall," *The Gardeners' Chronicle* (June 5, 1886):716.

96 Jancke, *Reise-Bericht*, 19–20.

97 Ibid., 22.

98 Ibid., 26.

99 "The apple yield is relatively higher than that of the pears. The varieties cultivated at *Knowsley* are, in the order in which they ripen, as follows . . . " (ibid., 29).

100 Ibid., 32–33.

101 Ibid., 35–36.

102 Ibid., 36.

103 Ibid., 37–42.

104 Ibid., 43–44.

105 Robson, "Peach Trees," 2. Similarly, *The Gardeners' Chronicle* reports in 1869 about Knowsley: "Ample provision has been made at Knowsley for the Vine, and, judging from the appearance of the Vines, there is good reason to believe that very fine Grapes will be grown there. Nothing likely to benefit the Vines seems to have been forgotten, and with the number of houses at command, there is little doubt that Mr. Freeman will be able to produce a splendid and continuous succession of Grapes throughout the year" (Wills, "Knowsley," 643). The author ends his article about Knowsley by apologizing: "As the cultivation of the Vine is to be one of the principal features of interest at Knowsley, I may be pardoned for wandering so far away from the subject which forms the heading of this paper" (644).

106 "Knowsley Hall," *The Gardeners' Chronicle* (June 5, 1886): 716.

107 Jancke, *Reise-Bericht*, 74.

108 Ibid., 44.

109 Ibid., 44ff.

110 Ibid., 58–59.

111 Cf. ibid., 66–68.

112 Ibid., 73; see his description of controlling the green peach aphid on p. 80.

113 Cf. ibid., 98; Brent Elliott raises the question whether the "use of liquid manure made from deer dung […] was supposed to be a particularly good manure, or was it an example of putting the other resources of Knowsley to good use, and wasting nothing?" (Brent Elliott, e-mail to author, August 29, 2012).

114 See, for example, "The arrangement of the Pine house, which is about 100 feet long by 30, seemed to be good. It was filled with Pines, while trellises round contained Cucumbers and Melons, and Strawberries were overhead" ("Knowsley Hall," *Journal of Horticulture and Cottage Gardener* [June 18, 1874]: 491–92). Or: "The cultivation of Pines appears as if it would almost die out altogether in this country but this noble fruit is still thought much of here. The principal house is some 45 feet by 30, and contains a fine lot of fruiting plants" ("Knowsley Hall," *The Gardeners' Chronicle* [June 5, 1886]: 716).

115 J. A., "The Pine Stove at Knowsley," *The Gardeners' Chronicle and Agricultural Gazette* February 11, 1865: 124.

116 Ibid., 124–25.

117 H. E., "Knowsley Hall," *The Gardeners' Chronicle* (October 25, 1890): 464.

118 Jancke, *Reise-Bericht*, 102–5.

119 Cf. ibid., 114–16.

120 Ibid., 117.

121 Ibid., 118–20.

REISE-BERICHT

HANS JANCKE

PLATE 1

PLATE 2

Inhalt.

———

PLATE 3

Sansfouci im Juni 1875.

Nachdem ich meine
durch den Krieg mit
Frankreich unterbrochenen
Studien in der
Königlichen Gärtner-
Lehranstalt, nach der
Rückkehr aus dem
Felde vollendet hatte,
gewährte mir Herr
Garten-Inspektor Gürdt
freundliche Aufnahme
in der von ihm gelei-
teten Gärtnerei des
Herrn Borsig; ich ar-
beitete dort ein Jahr
in den Orchideen-
und Warmhäusern.
Im Frühjahr 1873 ging
ich von dort nach Metz,
um mich daselbst in
der Baumschule von
Simon Louis Frères zu
beschäftigen und fand
im Herbst desselben
Jahres eine Stelle in
Linden's Etablissement
zu Gent. Daselbst ar-

PLATE 4

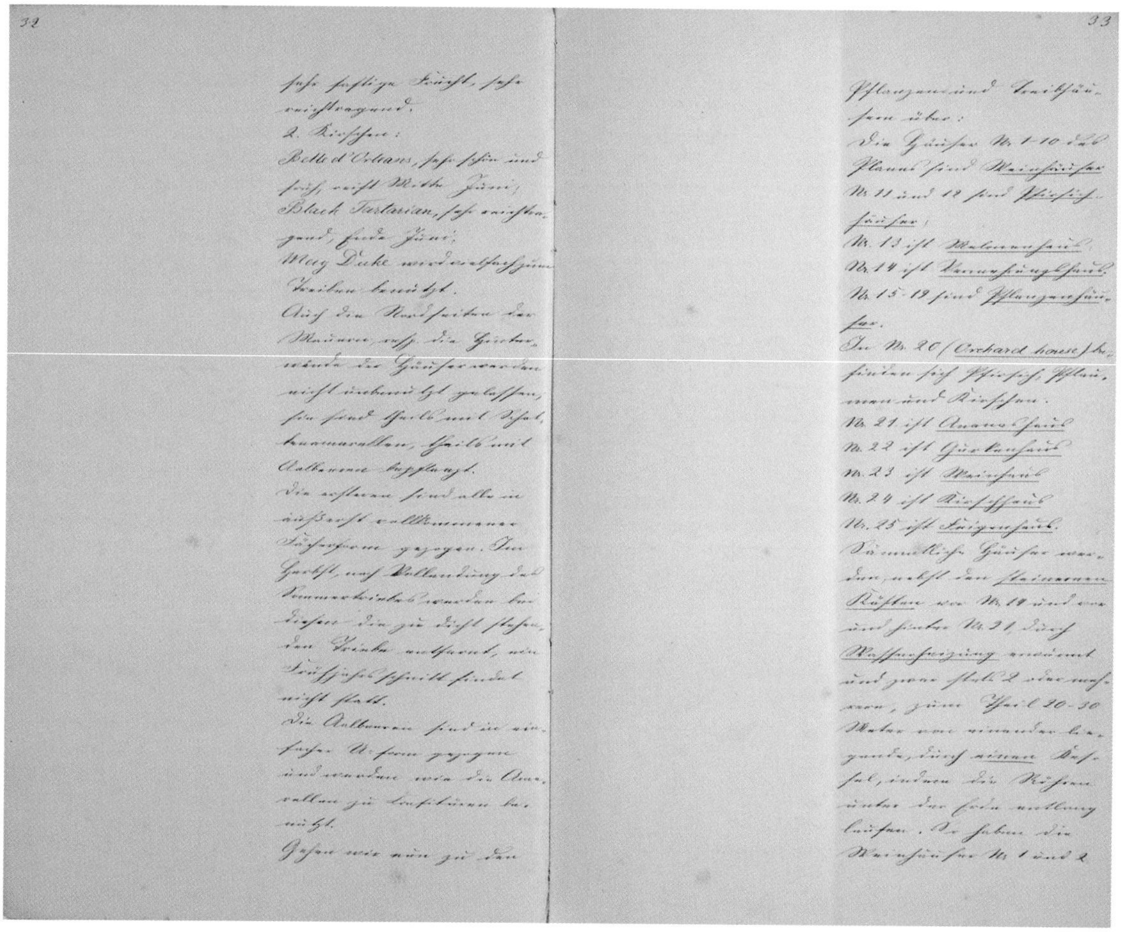
32

sehr saftige Frucht, sehr
reichtragend.
2. Kirschen:
Belle d'Orleans, sehr schön und
früh, reift Mitte Juni;
Black Tartarian, sehr reichtragend, Ende Juni;
May Duke wird ebenfalls zum
Treiben benützt.
Auf den Nordseiten der
Mauern, resp. die Giebel-
wände der Häuser werden
nicht unbenützt gelassen,
sie sind theils mit Schattenmorellen, theils mit
Aalbeeren bepflanzt.
Die ersteren sind alle in
äusserst vollkommener
Fächerform gezogen. Im
Herbst, nach Vollendung des
Sommertriebes werden bei
diesen die zu dicht stehenden Triebe entfernt, ein
Frühjahrsschnitt findet
nicht statt.
Die Aalbeeren sind in einfacher U-form gezogen
und werden wie die Ama-
rellen zu [illegible] be-
nützt.
Gehen wir nun zu den

33

Pflanzen- und Treibhäu-
sern über:
Die Häuser Nr. 1-10 des
Planes sind Weinhäuser
Nr. 11 und 12 sind Pfirsich-
häuser;
Nr. 13 ist Melonenhaus,
Nr. 14 ist Vermehrungshaus,
Nr. 15-19 sind Pflanzenhäu-
ser.
In Nr. 20 (Orchard house) be-
finden sich Pfirsich, Pflau-
men und Kirschen.
Nr. 21 ist Ananashaus
Nr. 22 ist Gurkenhaus
Nr. 23 ist Weinhaus
Nr. 24 ist Kirschhaus
Nr. 25 ist Feigenhaus.
Sämmtliche Häuser wer-
den, nebst den steinernen
Kästen vor Nr. 19 und vor
und hinter Nr. 21 durch
Wasserheizung erwärmt
und zwar stets 2 oder meh-
rere, zum Theil 20-30
Meter von einander lie-
gende, durch einen Kes-
sel, indem die Röhren
unter der Erde entlang
laufen. Wir haben die
Weinhäuser Nr. 1 und 2

INHALT

1 The lower right portion of the manuscript page is missing. The page numbers have been added in brackets.

S. 1

Sanssouci im Juni 1875
Nachdem ich meine durch den Krieg mit Frankreich unterbrochenen Studien in der Königlichen Gärtner-Lehranstalt, nach der Rückkehr aus dem Felde vollendet hatte, gewährte mir Herr Garten-Inspector *Gärdt*[2] freundliche Aufnahme in die von ihm geleitete Gärtnerei des Herrn *Borsig*; ich arbeitete dort ein Jahr in den Orchideen- und Wärmhäusern. Im Frühjahr 1873 ging ich von dort nach Metz, um mich daselbst in der Baumschule von *Simon Louis Frères* zu beschäftigen und fand im Herbst desselben Jahres eine Stelle in *Linden's* Etablissement zu Gent. Daselbst er-

S. 2

hielt ich im Februar 1874 die freudige Nachricht, daß mir durch hohes Wohlwollen ein Stipendium von 100 Thalern zur Reise nach England durch die Königliche Gärtner-Lehranstalt mit der Weisung zu Theil geworden, nach meiner Rückkehr über die dort gesammelten Erfahrungen Bericht zu erstatten. Durch freundliche Verwendung des Königlichen Obergärtners Herrn *Fintelmann* erhielt ich eine Stelle in den durch *Mr. Harrison* verwalteten *Knowsley-Gardens*, einer Besitzung des *Earl of Derby*, wo selbst ich vielfach Gelegenheit fand, meine Kenntnisse zu erweitern, worüber ich in Folgendem, der Aufgabe gemäß, Näheres zu berichten mir gehorsamst erlaube.

S. 3

Die <u>*Knowsley-Gardens*</u> liegen in dem schönsten Theile der regenreichen Grafschaft *Lancashire* inmitten blühender Dörfer und ausgedehnter Waldungen. Das Terrain ist sanft wellenförmig von Nordnordost nach Südsüdwest allmälig abfallend. Schöne alte Bäume, meist *Acer, Aesculus, Castanea, Fagus, Quercus, Tilia & Ulmus* überragen das dichte Unterholz, welches zum größten Theil aus immergrünen Gehölzen: *Ilex, Buxus,*

2 Hans Jancke primarily used Old German letters in the travel report; he used modern writing only for personal, place, and plant names. These terms are marked in italics in the transcription.

Cupressus, Thuja, Taxus und massenhaften *Rhododendron* bestehend, den Küchen-Obst- und Blumengarten, die Obst-Treibereien, Stallgebäude u. s. w. umgiebt, während jüngere Anpflanzungen, theils immergrüne, theils sommergrüne Bäume und Sträucher die wohlgepflegten, stets in safti-

S. 4

gem Grün prangenden Rasenflächen, welche das Schloss umgeben, angenehm unterbrechen. Das Seeclima mit seinen gelinden Wintern ermöglicht das Gedeihen einiger Exemplare von *Araucaria imbricata* und *Cedrus Deodara*, während die kühlen Sommer das Wachsthum von Gehölzen mit gefiederten Blättern nicht begünstigen, sie sind deshalb auch nur wenig vertreten, *Robinia, Gleditschia* und ähnliche fehlen gänzlich. Auch einige andere, bei uns sehr häufige Bäume sind nur sehr schwach vertreten, z. B. *Betula, Fraxinus, Platanus*. Bald nach meiner Ankunft in Knowsley regte sich in mir der Wunsch einen Plan von dem inneren Park zu besitzen, und als sich einer meiner Collegen erbot, mir beim Vermessen be-

S. 5

hülflich zu sein, machten wir uns nach Beschaffung einer Maßkette und eines Winkelkopfes—zum Ankauf einer Boussole oder eines Theodoliten, welche die Messung sehr erleichtert hätten, reichten meine Mittel nicht aus—ans Werk und hatten auch, fast täglich die freie Zeit nach Feierabend benutzend, bald etwa die Hälfte der vorgenommenen Arbeit vollendet. Nun ward mein Helfer behindert ferner mitzumessen, so daß ich auf mich allein angewiesen war. Anfangs hielt ich es für fast unmöglich, die angefangene Arbeit ohne Hülfe zu vollenden zumal ich auch meine freie Zeit benutzen mußte, um mir einerseits Notizen über die Treiberei zu machen, andererseits, um früher Gelerntes zu repetiren, aber

S. 6

schließlich brachte ich doch die Arbeit zu dem gewünschten Abschluß, so daß ich im Stande war, nach dem Croquis hier den Plan zu vollenden, welchen ich dem Bericht beifüge. Zum näheren Verständniß desselben erlaube ich mir folgende Erläuterungen:
Die *Knowsley-Gardens* sind von dem sie umschließenden *Knowsley-Park* durch eiserne Gitter vollständig abgeschlossen, welche hauptsächlich den Zweck haben, das Eindringen des zahlreichen Roth- und Damwildes zu verhindern. An zwei Seiten sind die *Gardens* durch Seen (A, B, C & D des Plans) begrenzt, welche sich weniger durch schöne Form als durch außerordentlich klares, reines Wasser und durch enormen Fischreichthum auszeichnen. Die an die *Gardens* grenzenden Häuser und Seeen

sind mit Mauerwerk eingefaßt, welches einen Theil des Umfassungsgitters
trägt.

Der See A, welcher den Garten im Osten begrenzt, ist etwa 600 Meter
lang und 250 Meter breit. Am gegenüber liegenden Ufer erhebt sich eine
Hügelreihe, welche im Sommer mit mit [*sic*] mannshohem Adlerfarn (*Pteris
aquilina*) bedeckt ist, das jährlich reichlich fructifirirt; aus diesem Grunde
erheben sich zahlreiche alte Nadel- und Laubbäume, welche von einem
alten ruinenhaften Thurm überragt werden. Der See gewährt von dem
Fischerhäuschen r, in welchem kostbare Boote zu Lustfahrten im Sommer
aufbewahrt werden, einen großartigen Anblick. Der See A liegt höher als
der größte Theil des Gartens

und versorgt denselben vermittelst eines vielverzweigten Röhrensystems mir
klarem, trinkbarem Wasser. Die am Ufer entlang laufenden Wege überragen
sein Niveau nur um wenige Meter. Der Wasserspiegel des Sees B liegt etwa
16 m tiefer als der von A, der von C liegt wiederum etwa 1,5 m tiefer als der
von B und der Spiegel von D liegt etwa 4 m tiefer als der von C; zu einer
genaueren Messung der Höhenunterschiede, welche ich sehr gern noch
vorgenommen hätte, fehlte mir leider die Zeit. Die genannten Seeen sind unter
sich und mit den vier kleineren in der Mitte des Gartens befindlichen Teichen
durch starke, unterirdische, abschließbare Röhren verbunden, durch welche
der im Frühjahr und schon zu Ende des Winters rasch steigende Wasserstand

regulirt wird. Der See D hat an seinem Westende einen Abfluß nach den
im Außenpark befindlichen Seeen [*sic*]. Fontainenanlagen sind, obgleich
sie mit großer Leichtigkeit und geringem Kostenaufwand hätten beschafft
werden können, noch nicht vorhanden, doch hat man, wie mir *Mr. Harrison*
mittheilte, die Absicht, in den nächsten Jahren an Stelle des großen Rhodo-
dendronbusches, welcher sich in der Mitte des umfangreichen, östlich
vom Schlosse gelegenen Blumenparterres befindet, einen Springbrunnen
herzustellen. Was die Bepflanzung des Parterres anbelangt, so werden von
den acht S-förmigen Beeten gewöhnlich vier mit einer Mitellinie [*sic*] von
Achyranthes Verschaffelti und einer Einfassung von *Pyrethrum*

Parthenium var. aureum bepflanzt, die anderen vier mit *Iresine Lindeni* und
Gnaphalium tomentosum als Einfassung. Die übrigen Beete werden mit

Siarlat-Pelargonien[3] bepflanzt und zwar bediente man sich im Sommer 1874 dazu folgender Spielarten:

Bonfire mit leuchtend zinnoberrother großer Blüte, kam nebst dem leuchtend mennigrothem

Warrior am meisten zur Verwendung, ferner:

Excellent fleischfarben,

Janthe carmoisinroth,

Blue Bell hellcarmoisinroth,

Thomas Speed zinnoberroth,

Jean Sisley mennigroth mit großem weißem Auge im Centrum,

Stella mit schmalblättrigen aber leuchtend dunkelrothen Blüthen,

Annie Hogg hellroth,

Mr Constance hell purpurfarben,

S. 11

Violet Hill fleischfarben.

Ferner kamen folgende buntblättrigen Varianten zur Verwendung:

Mrs. Pollock

Lady Cullum

Beauty of Caulderdale

Gem

Prince's Silver-Wing.

Mit goldgeränderten Blättern wurden verwendet:

Crystal Palace Gem,

Golden Chain,

mit silbergeränderten Blättern:

Silver Queen

Flower of Spring

Flower of the Day

Waltham Bride

Die mit Pelargonien bepflanzten Beete sind theils mit *Lobelia Erinus* theils mit *Gnaphalium lanatum*, theils mit *Echeveria metallica glauca* eingefaßt. Zur Bepflanzung der runden und elliptischen Beete zu beiden Seiten des Weges unmittelbar

S. 12

südlich vom Parterre werden folgende Pflanzen verwendet:

Ageratum Mexicanum Imperial Dwarf.

Calceolaria floribunda

Centaurea gymnocarpa

Lobelia Erinus

3 Although Jancke clearly wrote Siarlat in the travel report, it is unclear if today Scarlet-Pelargoniums would be meant.

Perilla Nankinensis

Tagetes patula

Heliotropium Peruvianum

ferner die schon oben genannten Pelargonien und verschiedene Petunien-Varietäten. Die beiden weiter zurückliegenden runden Gruppen enthalten *Canna Indica* und *Gladiolus* in vielen Varietäten.

Nördlich von dem besprochenen Parterre liegt das <u>Conservatory</u>, aus einer warmen und einer Camellien-Abtheilung bestehend und durch einen Corridor mit dem Schloß verbunden. In beiden Abtheilungen befinden sich je ein Mittelbeet und zwei Seiten-

S. 13

beete, in welchen zum Theil sehr schöne und werthvolle Pflanzen stehen. Unter den in der warmen Abtheilung befindlichen Pflanzen sind als empfehlenswerth hervorzuheben: Vier sehr starke Exemplare von *Musa Cavendishi*, welche jährlich Früchte liefern, 2 große Exemplare von *Cycas revoluta*, ferner

Hedychium Gardnerianum

Alpinia nutans

Bambusa gracilis

Coffea Arabica gleichfalls jährlich Früchte bringend,

Strelitzia ovata

Citrus Limonum

Plumbago Capensis

Clerodendron Balfouri

Bougainvillea glabra

Dipladenia amabilis

Thunbergia Harrissii

Passiflora quadrangularis & edulis, von Letzterer hatte ich einige Blüthen mit Pollen von *quadrangularis* befruchtet, welche auch

S. 14

sämmtlich Früchte ansetzten, die jedoch bei meiner Abreise leider noch nicht ganz reif waren. Ferner sind zu nennen:

Bactris Maraja

Kentia Balmoreana

Daemonorops melanochaetes

Euterpe edulis

Livistona Australis

Areca Verschaffelti

Ceroxylon niveum

Chamaedorea graminifolia
Salal umbraculifera
Welfia regia
Zalacca Wagneri
Sphaerogyne latifolia
Cyanophyllum magnificum
Pandanus Javanicus varieg.
     "   *graminifolius*
Hibiscus puniceus
Dichorisandra thyrsiflora
Euphorbia Jacquiniaeflora
Rivinia humilis
Rogiera cordata
Asclepias Curassavica
Stephanotis floribunda.
Die Hinterwand ist mit *Habrothamnus elegans* und *Clerodendron Balfouri*
bekleidet.

S. 15

Auf den Seitenbeeten befinden sich:
Gymnogramme sulphurea
     "   *ochracea*
     "   *Laucheana*
Neottopteris nidusavis
Doryopteris palmata
Asplenium Bellangeri
Cyrtomium falcatum
Pteris longifolia u. A.
Der Boden aller drei Beete ist mit *Selaginella denticulata, Oplismenes variegata,
Tradescantia zebrina, Fittonia argyroneura & rubrovenosa* dicht bewachsen.
Über den Wegen zu beiden Seiten des Mittelbeetes hängen zierliche aus Draht
geflochtene Ampeln, welche *Hoya bella, Ardisia crenata, Russellia juncea* etc
enthalten. Das Mittelbeet der kälteren Abteilung ist mit Camellien bepflanzt,
zur Bekleidung der Hinterwand dienen:

S. 16

Luculia gratissima
Acacia armata
     "   *oleifolia*
     "   *pubescens*
Habrothamnus elegans

Kennedya Maryatta und noch eine in *Knowsley* aus Samen gezogene Varietät von *Kennedya* mit üppigem Wuchs und schmutzigrothen Blüthen.

Als Schlingpflanze ist die schöne, hier leider noch so seltene *Tacsonia van Volxemii* vielfach verwendet. Auf den Seitenbeeten stehen: *Aspidium, Pteris, Scolopendrium* etc. zwischen welchen einige Exemplare von *Thea Bohea* und *Thea viridis* stehen, und außerdem, je nach Jahreszeit, verschiedene Topfgewächse Aufstellung finden: *Heliotropium, Fuchsia, Pelargonium, Chrysanthemum, Cytisus* etc.

Den Corridor zieren Camellien in Töpfen, ferner:

S. 17

Fuchisa und *Pelargonium, Lobelia fulgens, Acacia armata, Lapageria rosea & alba, Clianthus magnificus, Agave Americana* und *A. A. variegata*; die beiden Letzteren werden nie ins Freie gestellt.

Nördlich vom Schlosse befindet sich der <u>Küchengarten</u> mit wohlgepflegten Obstpflanzungen, Gewächs- und Treibhäusern, Mistbeeten u.s.w. Die nach Süden gelegenen Mauern des Küchengartens sind zur Hälfthe mit <u>Pfirsich-</u> zur anderen Hälfthe mit Aprikosen- und Birnenbäumen bekleidet.

Erstere sind durchweg in Fächerform erzogen und zwar in folgenden Sorten: *Noblesse,* frühtragend und zum Treiben sehr geeignet, *Royal George,* gleichfalls viel zum Treiben benutzt,

S. 18

Bellegarde, gleichfalls sehr empfehlenswerth, zum Versenden gut geeignet, da sie sich abgepflückt besser hält als die anderen Sorten, *Violette hâtive* reift im September, *Early Beatrice,* früh und sehr süß, *Salway, Dagmar & Walburton,* von den drei letzen waren nur junge Exemplare vorhanden, die noch keine Früchte trugen. An <u>Nectarinen</u> waren vorhanden: *Elruge,* sehr schön und zum Frühtreiben sehr geeignet, *Large Elruge* *Stanwick Elruge* *Pitmaston Orange* früh und reichtragend, August und September reifend, *Albert Victor,* schön und sehr groß, reift Anfang September. Von <u>Aprikosen</u> werden nur drei Sorten gezogen, nämlich: *Moorpark,* trägt reichlich

S. 19

schöne Früchte und ist jedenfalls eine der empfehlenswerthesten, *Turkey,* gleichfalls empfehlenswerth, Geschmack ein wenig säuerlich. *Persian Apricot.*

Die an Südmauern cultivirten <u>Birnen</u> sind, nach der Reifezeit geordnet, folgende:

Williams's bon chrétien, lieferte bereits im August vorzügliche Früchte in großer Anzahl,

British Queen, September,

Duchesse d'Angoulême, trug im vorigem Jahr in *Knowsley* nur wenige und nicht sehr schöne Früchte, soll überhaupt, wie man mir sagte, nur in besonders warmen Jahren dort einen guten Ertrag liefern,

Gansels Bergamot, trug keine guten Früchte,

Marie Louise wurde im reichen Tragen nur von *Glout Morceau* übertroffen, während sich an Güte

S. 20

wohl beide gleichstanden,

B. Diel liefert auch in *Knowsley* große Früchte.

Passe Colmar liefert an den Mauern einen guten Ertrag.

Glout Morceau ist eine der in *Lancashire* am höchsten geschätzten Winterbirnen, liefert einen außerordentlich reichen Ertrag von großen, feinen Früchten, die sich sehr lange halten.

Winter Nélis, gleichfalls eine vorzügliche Winterbirn,

Ne plus meuris reift im März,

Beurré de Rance hält sich bis zum Mai.

Die Ostmauern sind ausschließlich für Birnen benutzt und zwar befinden sich an denselben folgende Sorten, gleichfalls nach der Reifezeit geordnet:

Williams's bon chrétien

Jargonelle, gut,

Summer Frank Real trägt

S. 21

zwar nur kleine aber sehr saftige und süße Früchte,

Beurré d'Amanlis, wohl eine der besten Sommerbirnen,

Beurré superfin, groß und gut,

Beurré de Capiaumont, reich tragend,

Aston Town mit kleinen aber schönen Früchten, gleichfalls reichtragend,

Duchesse d'Angoulême

Thompsons, gut,

Gansels Bergamot,

Crassanne an den Mauern gut tragend,

Forelle reichtragend, schön gefärbt,

Winter Nélis,

Josephine de Malines, gut,

Easter Beurré gut an den Mauern,

Baronne de Mello, groß und gut,

Außerdem befanden sich an den Altmauern einige junge Bäume, die noch
nicht trugen:

Black Styrian,

Moccas,

S. 22

Knight's Monarch.

Wenn auch an den gegen Osten gelegenen Mauern die Birnen an Geschmack
und Größe den an den Südmauern stehenden nicht völlig gleichkamen, so
übertrafen sie doch die in Pyramidenform gezogenen ganz merklich, was
namentlich bei *Passe Colmar, Cassanne* und *Glout Morceau* auffiel.

An den Mauern waren einige wenige Bäume in Fächerform und in schiefästiger
Palmettenform, alle übrigen als Horizontalpalmetten gezogen.

Die Birnen in Pyramidenform befinden sich auf den schmalen Beeten
zu beiden Seiten der Wege des Küchengartens, wo sie mit Apfelbäumen
abwechseln. Es wurden als Pyramiden in *Knowsley* folgende Sorten
cultivirt:

Doyonné d'Été, trug am besten von den Sommerbirnen,

S. 23

Jargonelle, sehr empfehlenswerth, begann in diesem Jahre schon Ende Januar
zu treiben,

Williams's bon chrétien

Brockworth Park

British Queen

Beurré d'Amanlis

Doyenné blanc, schön, reichtragend,

Fondante d'Automne, eine der besten Birnen für den October,

Jersey Gratioli

Baronne de Mello

Swan's Egg

Louise bonne de Jersey sehr schön und sehr reichtragend,

Duchesse d'Angoulême

Marie Louise, wenn auch als Pyramide nicht schön wachsend, so doch gute
Erträge liefernd,

Comte de Lamy, sehr gut,

Délices d'Hardenpont, gut, schön und reichtragend,

Passe Colmar, als Pyramide weniger gut als an den Mauern,

Crassanne,

Colmar d'Aremberg, sehr grobkörnig,

Glout Monceau, wenn auch nicht ganz so gut, wie an den Mauern, so doch im Wohlgeschmack immer noch mit allen anderen wetteifernd und die meisten an Tragbarkeit übertreffend,

Doyenné du Comice trug nur wenige, doch sehr gute Früchte.

Huyshe's Victoria

Alexandre Lambre

Winter Nélis

Zephirin Grégoire hat ein sehr schönes Aroma, Früchte klein,

General Todtleben

Bellissime d'hiver

Von *Délices de Jodoigne* und *Huyshe's Bergamot* waren viele junge, noch nicht tragende Pyramiden vorhanden.

Außer diesen, an Mauern und als Pyramiden gezogenen, wurden auch Birnen an freistehenden Spalieren gezogen, welche sich zu beiden Seiten

des durch den Küchengarten führenden Hauptweges befinden und zwar folgende Sorten:

Beurré superfin

Beurré Hardy

Swan's Egg

Louise bonne de Jersey trug sehr reichlich schöne Früchte

Flemish Beauty, gleichfalls gut,

Jersey Gratioli

Duchesse d'Angoulême

Marie Louise, auch hier vorzüglich und reichtragend,

Jalousie de Fontenay

Passe Colmar trug schlecht,

Triomphe de Jodoigne

Délices d'Hardenpont, gut,

Colmar d'Aremberg

Napoléon, gut,

Prince of Wales

Glout Morceau vorzüglich wie an den Mauern

Hacons Incomparable

Colmar, hier nicht so gut wie an den Mauern,

Winter Beurré trug reichlich kleine Früchte von schönem Aroma,

Winter Nélis, sehr schön,

S. 26

Josephine de Malines brachte eine reiche Ernte vorzüglicher Früchte.
Von *Suffolk Thorn* war ein junger Baum vorhanden, der noch nicht trug,
wird als gut empfohlen. Wenn der Ertrag an Birnen in *Knowsley* den
Erträgen, wie sie in Belgien und namentlich Frankreich und Lothringen
erzielt werden, nicht gleichkommt, so ist wohl der Grund hierfür nur in
dem feuchten Klima, den wenig warmen Sommern zu suchen[,] auch ist die
Ernte immerhin noch eine solche, daß man sich für die aufgebotenen Mittel
und die angewendete Mühe als belohnt erachten kann. Den Ertrag mancher
an den Mauern stehenden Sorten kann man geradezu einen sehr reichen
nennen, weniger gut war der an den freistehenden Spalieren, wenn auch
immerhin noch größer als der von den pyrami-

S. 27

denförmig gezogenen Bäumen.
Der Boden ist in *Knowsley* im Allgemeinen ein schwerer, humusreicher
Lehmboden, welcher durch eine vorzügliche Drainage für Obstkulturen
geeigneter gemacht ist. Die Birnen sind, wie schon gesagt, meist in
Horizontalpalmettenform und in Pyramidenform gezogen, der Schnitt ist
im Allgemeinen derselbe wie hier. Mit dem Frühjahrsschnitt beginnt man
Ende Januar. Die Leitzweige werden zur Erzielung guten Fruchtholzes
durchschnittlich länger als bei uns geschnitten, da das feuchte Clima und
der schwere Boden weniger den Fruchtansatz als vielmehr den Holztrieb
begünstigen; aus demselben Grunde wird auch an Mauern und Spalieren
die Horizontalpalmette allen anderen Formen vorge-

S. 28

zogen; da ja die horizontale Lage der Zweige den Fruchtansatz sehr
begünstigt.
Im Mai werden die Spitzen der jüngeren Triebe ausgekniffen.
Im August werden die Sommertriebe etwa auf die Hälfthe ihrer
Längen zurückgeschnitten, wodurch sich die Knospen zu den unteren
Hälften zu Blatt und Blüthenknospen entwickeln. Im October werden
die Fruchtruthen auf 4–5 Augen, die zu starken sogar auf Astring
zurückgeschnitten.
Wie schon oben erwähnt, befinden sich außer den Birnenpyramiden
auch Apfelbäume, zum Theil in hochstämmiger, zum Theil in niedriger
Pyramidenform, zum Theil auch in Kesselform erzogen, auf den Beeten
zu beiden Seiten der Wege im Küchengarten, auch befinden sich an
einigen

S. 29

Beeten Einfassungen von <u>Apfelbäumen</u>, welche als Horizontale Cordons gezogen sind; der Schnitt derselben unterscheidet sich, wie bei den Birnen, von dem hier angewendeten im Prinzip nicht.

Der Ertrag an Äpfeln ist verhältnißmäßig ein reicherer als der an Birnen. Die Sorten, welche in *Knowsley* cultivirt werden, sind, der Reifezeit nach geordnet, folgende:

Early Hearvest, sehr gut, bereits Ende Juli reifend,

Lord Suffield guter Wirthschaftsapfel,

Duchess of Oldenburgh, mittelgroß, von schönem Geschmack,

Summer Golden Pipin, sehr gut, in Guirlandenform gezogen,

White Astrachan, sehr gut,

Scarlet Parmain

Cellini

Gravenstein, sehr gut,

Hawthornden, großer Wirthschaftsapfel,

S. 30

King of Pippins, gut, reichtragend,

Flower of Kent, großer Wirthschaftsapfel, reichtragend,

Franklin's golden Pippin

Essex Pippin, klein,

Beauty of Kent, groß und von schönem Aussehen, aber nicht sehr wohlschmeckend,

Ribston Pippin, sehr reichtragend,

Northern Spy sehr gut,

Lord Derby, großer Wirthschaftsapfel,

Cox's Orange Pippin, schön und wohlschmeckend,

Blenheim orange Pippin, groß und gut als Pyramide und als Guirlande,

Court pendu plat gut, reichtragend,

Lewis's incomparable, groß,

Rosemary Russet, sehr schön,

Golden Russet, sehr wohlschmeckend,

Dutch Mignonne, von schönem Aroma, reichtragend,

Cornish Gilliflower als Cordonbäumchen gezogen,

Scarlet Nonpareil

White Calville, trägt in

S. 31

Knowlsey keine guten Früchte,

Old Nonpareil, reichtragend,

Boston Russet, sehr gut.

Die Westmauern des Küchengartens sind mit Pflaumen- und Kirschbäumen bepflanzt und zwar mit folgenden Sorten:

1. Pflaumen:

Green Gage (Frühe Reineclaude) reift in den Mauern Mitte August.

Coe's late red mit kleinen rothen, nicht sehr schönen Früchten, reifte erst im November,

Jefferson trug reichlich große, gelbe, rothpunktirte, sehr süße Früchte und reifte wie alle folgenden im September,

Denyers Victoria

Coe's golden drop trug sehr schöne und wohlschmeckende Früchte in großer Menge,

Transparent Gage, mit großer, schöner Frucht von gutem Geschmack,

Kukes plum, große, blaue

S. 32

sehr saftige Früchte, sehr reichtragend.

2. Kirschen:

Belle d'Orleans, sehr schön und früh, reift Mitte Juni,

Black Tartarian, sehr reichtragend, Ende Juni,

May Duke wird vielfach zum Treiben benutzt.

Auch die Nordseiten der Mauern, resp. die Hinterwände der Häuser werden nicht unbenutzt gelassen; sie sind theils mit Schattenmorellen, theils mit Aalbeeren bepflanzt.

Die ersteren sind alle in äußerst vollkommener Fächerform gezogen. Im Herbst, nach Vollendung des Sommertriebes werden bei diesen die zu dicht stehenden Triebe entfernt, ein Frühjahrsschnitt findet nicht statt.

Die Aalbeeren sind in einfacher U-Form gezogen und werden wie die Amarellen zu Confitüren benutzt.

Gehen wir nun zu den

S. 33

Pflanzen- und Treibhäusern über:

Die Häuser Nr 1–10 des Planes sind <u>Weinhäuser</u>

Nr 11 und 12 sind <u>Pfirsichhäuser</u>,

Nr. 13 ist <u>Melonenhaus</u>,

Nr. 14 ist <u>Vermehrungshaus</u>

Nr 15–19 sind <u>Pflanzenhäuser</u>.

In Nr. 20 (*Orchard house*) befinden sich Pfirsich, Pflaumen und Kirschen.

Nr. 21 ist <u>Ananashaus</u>

Nr. 22 ist <u>Gurkenhaus</u>

Nr. 23 ist <u>Weinhaus</u>
Nr. 24 ist <u>Kirschhaus</u>
Nr. 25 ist <u>Feigenhaus</u>.
Sämmtliche Häuser werden, nebst den <u>steinernen Kästen</u> vor Nr. 14 und vor
und hinter Nr. 21, durch <u>Wasserheizung</u> erwärmt und zwar stets 2 oder mehrere,
zum Theil 20–30 Meter von einander liegende, durch <u>einen</u> Kessel, indem die
Röhren unter der Erde entlang laufen. So haben die Weinhäuser Nr 1 und 2

S. 34

eine gemeinschaftliche Feuerung, ebenso Nr. 3 und 4. Durch die Feuerung
hinter Nr. 5 werden die Häuser Nr. 5 und 6 geheizt, während ein großer Kessel
(hinter Nr. 9) die Weinhäuser Nr 7, 8 & 9, das Kirschhaus Nr. 24 und das
Feigenhaus Nr. 25 mit Wärme versorgt.
Die Heizung für das Pfirsichhaus Nr. 12, das Gurkenhaus Nr. 13, das Ananashaus,
den davor und einen dahinter liegenden Kasten, befindet sich hinter Nr. 12.
Hinter Nr. 10 liegt der Kessel, durch welchen die Weinhäuser Nr. 11 und 12, das
Kalthaus Nr 14 und die davor liegenden Kästen geheizt werden, während sich
die Heizung für das Vermehrungshaus Nr. 15, die Kalthäuser Nr. 16 und 17, das
Gurkenhaus Nr. 22 und das Weinhaus Nr. 23 zwischen Nr. 16 und 17 befindet.
Für die Orchideen- und Warmhäuser Nr. 18 und 19, sowie

S. 35

sowie [sic] den davor liegenden Kasten befindet sich die Heizung hinter Nr. 18.
Von den beiden <u>Pflanzenhäusern</u> Nr. 18 und 19 ist ersteres das wärmere
und befinden sich darin namentlich Pflanzen aus Ost-Indien und von den
Südseeinseln, bemerkenswerth sind darunter:
Aerides Fieldingii
     "   *odoratum*
     "   *quinquevulnerum*
     "   *Schroederi*
     "   *suavissimum*
     "   *virens*
Angrecum eburneum
Porassia brachyata
Goodyera Dawsoniana
Phalaenopsis amabilis
     "   *grandiflora aurea*
     "   *Schilleriana*
Renanthera coccinea
Saccolabium Blumei
     "   *giganteum*

Vanda Batemanni
    "   gigantea
    "   Lowii
    "   Roxburghii

S. 36

Vanda suavis
    "   teres
    "   tricolor
Nepenthes ampullacea
    "   Phyllamphora
    "   Rafflesiana
Croton irregulare
    "   interruptum
    "   majesticum
    "   maximum
    "   spirale
    "   undulatum
    "   Veitchii
    "   Weissmanni
Ataccia cristata
Dracaena amabilis
    "   Cooperi
    "   Guilfolei
    "   reginae
    "   Youngei
Clerodendron Balfourei
    "   fallax
Anthurium leuconeurum
    "   magnificum
    "   pedato-radiatum
    "   regale
    "   Scherzerianum
Allocasia metallica
Sonerilla margaritacea
etc. etc. etc.
In Nr 19 befinden sich fol-

S. 37

gende bemerkenswerthe Pflanzen:
Ada aurantiaca

Calanthe Masuca
      "   *Veitchii*
      "   *veratrifolia*
      "   *vestita*
Cattleya Aclandiae
      "   *bicolor*
      "   *Forbesii*
      "   *Gigas*
      "   *labiata*
      "   *maxima*
      "   *Mossiae*
      "   "   *superba*
      "   *quadricolor*
      "   *Skinneri*
      "   *Trianaei*
      "   *Wagneri*
Coelogyne aistata
Cymbidium giganteum
Cypripedium barbatum
      "   *barbatum majus*
      "   *concolor*
      "   *hirsutum*
      "   *Hookerii*
      "   *insigne*
      "   *Javanicum*
      "   *niveum*
      "   *Pearcei*
      "   *Roezlei*

S. 38

Cypripedium Stonei
      "   *venustum*
      "   *villosum*
Selenipedium caudatum
      "   *Schlimii*
Dendrobium chrysanthum
      "   *Dalhousianum*
      "   *densiflorum*
      "   *Devonianum*
      "   *Farmerii*

      "   fimbriatum oculatum

      "   infundibilum

      "   macranthum

      "   nobile

      "   Paxtoni

Epidendrum aurantiacum

      "   ciliare

      "   fragrans

      "   prismatocarpum

Houlletia Brocklehourstiana

Laelia acuminata

      "   anceps

      "   autumnalis

      "   crispa

      "   majalis

      "   purpurea

Leptotes bicolor

Lycaste Skinneri

Masdevallia ignea

Maxillaria picta

      "   venusta

S. 39

Mesopinidium sanguineum

      "   vulcanium

Miltonia candida

      "   Moreliana purpurea

      "   spectabilis

Odontoglossum Alexandrae

      "   Bictoniense

      "   citrosmum

      "   Ehrenbergii

      "   gloriosum

      "   grande

      "   Insleayi

      "   Pescatorei

      "   Phalaenopsis

      "   pulchellum

      "   triumphans

      "   vexillarium

Oncidium ampliatum
  " *bifolium*
  " *cucullatum*
  " *Lanceanum*
  " *ornithorrhynchum*
  " *sphacelatum*
  " *uniflorum*
Phajus grandifolius
  " *maculatus*
  " *Wallichii*
Pilumna fragrans
Pleione humilis
  " *maculata*
Polycyenis barbata

S. 40

Sobralia macrantha
  " *violacea*
Sophronites grandiflora
Trichopilia coccinea
  " *suavis*
  " *tortilis*
Zygopetalum Mackayi
  " *maxillare*
Ferner die schon oben genannten *Croton* und *Dracaena*
Maranta Legrelleana
  " *illustris*
  " *Chimboracensis*
  " *Mackoyana*
  " *hieroglyphica*
  " *tubispatha*
  " *Veitchii*
  " *princeps*
  " *regalis*
  " *vittata*
  " *setosa*
  " *cinerea*
  " *discolor*
  " *amabilis*
  " *argyrea*
  " *eximia*

    "   micans
    "   Lindeni
    "   fasciata
    "   roseopicta
    "   Wallisii

S. 41

Maranta virginalis major
    "   *zebrina*
    "   *van den Heckii*
    "   *splendida*
    "   *smaragdina*
Aphelandra aurantiaca
Aralia leptophylla
    "   *reticulata*
Bilbergia zebrina
Nidularium fulgens
Tillandria Lindeni
    "   *musaica*
    "   *tesselata*
Vriesia psittacina
Calamus ciliaris
Cocos Weddeliana
Pandanus Veitchii
Coccoloba plalyclada
Cyrtanthera chrysostephana
Dalechampia Roezleana
Dipladenia amabilis
Epiphyllum truncatum an Draht gezogen 8m lang.
Eranthemum pulchellum
Eucharis Amazonica
Franciscea confertiflora
Garcinia Livingstonii
Gardenia citriodora
    "   *Fortunei*
    "   *radicans*
Hibiscus puniceus

S. 42

Ixora coccinea
Pancratium fragrans

Pentas Kermesina
Phyllotaenium Lindenii
Tabernomontana coronaria
Thyrsacanthus rutilans
Außerdem findet in Nr. 19 eine schöne Collection von Caladien Ausstellung:
Caladium argyrites
      "   *Auber*
      "   *Beethoven*
      "   *Belleymii*
      "   *Brogniardtii*
      "   *Chantini*
      "   *Meyerbeer*
      "   *Prince Albert Edward*
      "   *Wrightii, etc.*
Die gemauerten Kästen und die Kalthäuser dienen zur zeitweiligen Aufnahme von *Erica, Poinsettia, Pelargonium, Cineraria, Calceolaria, Bouvardia* etc. In den <u>Treibhäusern</u> werden folgende Früchte getrieben:
Wein, Pfirsich, Ananas, Kirschen, Feigen, Gurken. Zur Erdbeeren und Bohnentreiberei werden die an-

S. 43

deren Treibhäuser mitbenutzt. Viele von den Häusern, namentlich von den neueren, sind durchaus musterhaft construirt und habe ich mir deshalb von einigen derselben genaue Zeichnungen angefertigt, welche ich den einzelnen Capiteln über die Treiberei verschiedener Obstarten beifüge. Den ersten Rang in der Obsttreiberei nimmt in *Knowsley*
<u>die Weintreiberei</u>
ein. Da das Clima des nördlichen Englands die Cultur des Weinstocks im Freien nicht erlaubt, wird daselbst auf die Weintreiberei außerordentliche Sorgfalt verwendet und die dadurch erzielten Erfolge sind so bedeutend, daß die dort erzogenenen Trauben denjenigen anderer Länder, deren Clima die Weincultur weit mehr begünstigst, an Größe,

S. 44

Färbung und Wohlgeschmack nicht nur nicht nachstehen, sondern sie sogar übertreffen.
In den Königlichen Gärten sowie in denen reicher Privatleute und in zahlreichen Handelsgärtnereien Englands werden durch frühzeitiges Antreiben die ersten reifen Trauben im März erzielt und, da sich die am spätesten reifenden Sorten bei einiger Sorgfalt bis zu dieser Zeit conserviren lassen, hat man das ganze Jahr hindurch reife Weintrauben.

Fig. A1 zeigt den Durchschnitt des in den *Knowsley-Gardens* zum ersten Weintreiben verwendeten Hauses (Plan Nr. 23; Fig. A2 = Plan Nr. 22 ist das Gurkenhaus). Die Erwärmung des Hauses geschieht hier, wie fast durchweg in England durch Wasserheizung. Bei A in Figur A tritt das aus dem oberen Theil das Kessels K kommende, heiße Was-

S. 45

ser ein, giebt einen großen Theil seiner Wärme an die eisernen Röhren und an das Haus ab, wird durch seine Abkühlung schwerer und fließt durch die allmälig bis b sich senkende Röhre zurück in den unteren Theil des Kessels, worin es, von Neuem erhitzt, wiederum in die Höhe steigt und den Kreislauf fortsetzt.

Auf den eisernen Röhren befinden sich die Behälter c,c,c, welche mit Wasser gefüllt werden, und durch dessen Verdampfung eine gleichmäßig feuchte Luft im Hause zu erhalten. (Vergleiche Figur B, welche den Grundriß des Hauses nebst Heizungsröhren und Kessel, von oben gesehen, darstellt.).

Die Röhren d in Fig. A dienen dazu, beim Füllen der Heizungsröhren mit Wasser der Luft den Austritt zu ermöglichen.

S. 46

Das Wasser im Reservoir e dient dazu, durch die Röhren f die Heizröhren stets gefüllt zu halten. Die im Reservoir auf dem Wasser schwimmende kupferne Hohlkugel g ist durch den Arm k mit dem leicht drehbaren Hahn i verbunden; sinkt der Wasserstand in e, so sinkt damit zugleich die Kugel und öffnet dadurch den Hahn, durch diese Vorrichtung wird also stets eine gewisse Höhe des Wasserstandes im Reservoir erhalten, die man durch Biegen des Armes h nach Belieben verändern kann. Man findet diese praktische Vorrichtung auch an allen Bassins im Inneren der Häuser; durch den fortwährenden langsamen Zufluß wird das Wasser stets in einer möglichst gleichmäßigen Temperatur erhalten, welche der des Hauses nahe kommt.

z in Fig. B sind Hähne durch deren völliges oder

S. 47

theilweises Oeffnen oder Schließen die Temperatur der Häuser mit Leichtigkeit auf's Genauste geregelt werden kann. y in Figur B sind Wasserreservoire.

Das Luftgeben geschieht vermittelst der Vorrichtungen m und n in Figur A, l ist der Gang zwischen den Beeten u, welche zur Aufnahme der Weinstöcke dienen. Die Beete werden mit Laub und Pferdemist gefüllt, wohinein man die in Töpfen stehenden Weinstöcke füttert. Auf dem Boden der Beete befinden sich zur nachhaltigeren Erwärmung eiserne Röhren (o & p in Figg. A & B) welche gleichfalls durch heißes Wasser aus dem Kessel K erwärmt werden. Fig. C ist ein senkrechter Durchschnitt des Kessels K, die Röhren

S. 48

a b o & p entsprechen den gleichbenannten in Figg. A und B.
Durch die Röhren q, r, s und t werden die Häuser 15, 16 und 17 des Planes geheizt.
Fig. D ist der Grundriß eines Stückes des in Fig. A mit v bezeichneten Läufers, ähnliche Läufer finden in englischen Häusern vielfach Verwendung. Zum Frühtreiben werden junge, in Töpfen stehende Weinstöcke benutzt, welche, nachdem sie getragen haben, fortgeworfen werden. Ihre Anzucht geschieht aus Augen.
Die Augen von kräftigen, im Spätherbst oder Winter geschnittenen Reben werden so herausgeschnitten, daß ihnen zu beiden Seiten etwa 1,5 Centimeter Holz bleiben. An der dem Auge entgegengesetzten Seite wird

S. 49

⅓ des Holzes, der Länge nach, glatt abgeschnitten (Siehe Fig. E). Man schneidet die Augen in der ersten Hälfte des Januar und legt sie so gleich in einen mit Flußsand gefüllten, und mit gutem Abzug versehenen Kasten so, wagerecht hinein, daß nur das Auge selbst die Oberfläche des Sandes überragt, und daß jedes Auge vom anderen einen Abstand von 4–5 Centimetern hat.
Der Kasten wird an einen warmen Platz (Gurkenhaus) gestellt. Sobald die Augen 6–10 Centimeter lang ausgetrieben, werden sie in Töpfen von 4–5 ctm Weite gepflanzt, in eine Mischung von sandigem Lehm, Composterde und Kalkschutt. Wenn sie gut durchgewurzelt, pflanzt

S. 50

man sie in 10 und später in 20 ctm weite Töpfe, in welchen sie bis zum nächsten Jahr bleiben. Bei Eintritt warmer Witterung finden sie im Freien, an einer Südmauer Aufstellung. Wenn das Holz gut reif geworden ist, schneidet man die Reben bis auf 1–2 Augen zurück und hält sie den Winter über frostfrei. Im nächsten Frühjahr, wenn die Augen 4–5 Centimeter lang ausgetrieben haben und zugleich die Wurzeln in vollem Wachsen sind, werden die Stöcke in 30 ctm weite Töpfe verpflanzt in eine Mischung von sandigem Lehm, Composterde, Kalkschutt und Knochenmehl. Nur der stärkste Trieb wird am Stock belassen, der andere eingestutzt und später fortgeschnitten. Sobald die Töpfe gut durchwurzelt, erhalten sie wöchentlich 1–2 Mal einen

S. 51

Dungguß und werden den Sommer über an einem geschützten, sonnigen
Platz aufgestellt.

Nach vollendeter Holzreife werden die Reben auf 1–2 Meter
zurückgeschnitten und Ende October in die dazu mit Mist und Laub
vorbereiteten Beete gebracht (Fig. A).

Um ein gleichmäßiges Austreiben der sämmtlichen Augen zu bewirken
und namentlich die oberen Augen zum Nutzen der mittleren und unteren
möglichst zurückzuhalten wird (Fig. F1.) die Rebe heruntergebunden.

Sobald die Töpfe ins Haus genommen sind, wird das Gießen mit Dungwasser
vorläufig eingestellt. Die Temperatur für die erste Woche beträgt bei Tage 12
und bei Nacht 8°R.[4] Die Luft des Hauses wird durch Besprengen des Bodens
und der Wände sowie

S. 52

durch Anfüllen der auf den Heizröhren befindlichen Wasserbehälter
(*evaporating pans*) gleichmäßig feucht gehalten, die Weinstöcke selbst
werden Morgens und Nachmittags mit 18–20° warmen Wasser überspritzt.
Die Temperatur wird nun allmälig auf 16° bei Tage und 12° bei Nacht erhöht,
bei Sonnenschein kann sie stets 4–5° höher steigen. Sobald sich die Augen
geöffnet, und einen bis zwei Centimeter ausgetrieben haben, bindet man die
Reben sorgfältig an das Spalier (*w* in Fig. A). Wenn sich die Trauben deutlich
entwickelt haben, hört man mit Spritzen auf und feuchtet nur noch Wände
und Fußboden an. Man läßt jedem Stock nur 3–4 gut entwickelte Trauben,
zwei Augen über der Traube wird der Trieb pincirt. Während der Blüthezeit
hält man die Temperatur auf 18°R bei Tage und

S. 53

und 14° bei Nacht und giebt ein wenig mehr Luft um die Befruchtung zu
befördern, dabei darf man aber die Luft im Hause nicht zu trocken werden
lassen. Bald nach dem Abblühen beginnt man mit dem Ausbeeren. Man
schneidet mit der Schere durchschnittlich den dritten Theil der Beeren
heraus, um den übrigen mehr Platz zu gewähren und ihnen zugleich mehr
Nahrung zuzuführen. Mit Bastfäden werden die oberen Zweige der Trauben
sorgfältig hoch und auseinander gebunden, damit sich die einzelnen Beeren,
ohne sich gegenseitig zu berühren, recht vollkommen entwickeln können.
Nach dem Abblühen gießt man die Töpfe wiederum wöchentlich einmal mit
Dungwasser, welches aus Hirschmist bereitet wird. Sobald sich die Beeren zu
färben be-

4 Jancke used the
Réaumur temperature
scale. 12°Réaumur
equals 15° Celsius.

S. 54

ginnen, was Ende März der Fall ist, wird das Gießen mit Dungwasser eingestellt und die Temperatur auf 16° bei Tage und 12° bei Nacht erniedrigt und so bis zur Reifezeit beibehalten. Während dieser ganzen Periode, vom Beginn des Färbens bis zur Reife hält man das Haus ziemlich trocken und giebt reichlich Luft, auch bei Nacht wird dieselbe nicht ganz fortgenommen. Man erzielt durch dies reichliche Lüften eine gute Farbe und ein schönes Aroma. Haben die Trauben vollständige Reife erlangt, so hält man durch reichliches Lüften das Haus kühl und trocken, um die Ernte der Trauben möglichst zu verlängern. Nachdem die Trauben abgenommen sind werden die Weinstöcke fortgeworfen.

Die besten und in England am meisten zum Frühtreiben benutzten Weinsorten

S. 55

sind: *Black Hamburgh* und *Foster's Seedling,* erstere nimmt unter den blauen, letztere unter den weißen Sorten zum Frühtreiben unbedingt die erste Stelle ein.

Black Hamburg liefert mittelgroße Trauben mit mittelgroßen Beeren und ist sehr empfehlenswerth,

Foster's Seedling trägt mittelgroße Trauben von 3–4 lb. Schwere, die Beeren sind gleichfalls mittelgroß, zart gelb und sehr wohlschmeckend. In den Häusern, welche zum zweiten und späteren Treiben benutzt werden, stehen die Weinstöcke im Bande. Zur Anzucht werden Ende Februar oder Anfang März gute Augen von starken Reben in vorbeschriebener Weise gesteckt und ebenso den nächsten Sommer und Winter über behandelt.

Im folgenden Frühjahr werden die Stöcke in das für sie bestimmte Haus

S. 56

Haus [*sic*] gepflanzt, nachdem der schwere Lehmboden 1 Meter tief rigolt und reichlich mit Kalkschutt und Knochenmehl gemischt ist. Unter jeden Sparren und unter die Mitte eines jeden Fensters wird je ein Stock gepflanzt, so daß die Entfernung der Pflanzen von einander etwa 0,75 Meter beträgt.

Ist die Nordmauer des Hauses durchbrochen gebaut (siehe Fig: F) so daß die Wurzeln nach Außen durchdringen können, was bei Häusern zum späten Treiben sehr zu empfehlen ist, so pflanzt man die Stöcke 0,3–0,5 Meter von derselben entfernt, bei Häusern mit solider Vordermauer dagegen (wie Haus Fig. G) bleibt man 1–1,5 m zurück, damit sich die Wurzeln nach allen Seiten ausbreiten können. Sobald die Augen ausgetrieben haben, läßt man jedem Weinstock nur einen Trieb. Den Sommer über wird reichlich gespritzt und gelüftet und die Geiztriebe auf 2 Blätter gestutzt. Sobald im Herbst die völlige Holzreife eingetreten ist, zu deren Erlangung man bei kühlem, trübem Herbstwetter heizt, so schneidet man die Reben je nach ihrer Stärker auf 0,5–1m zurück und überwintert sie frostfrei. Von den im nächsten Frühjahr wachsenden Seitentrieben läßt man so viele am Stock, daß sie an jeder Seite etwa 0,3m von einander entfernt stehen. Später werden die Seitentriebe auf 0,5 Meter gestutzt während man den Endtrieb ungehindert wachsen läßt, um ihn nach eingetretener Holzreife wieder auf 05,–1m zu stutzen. Die Seitentriebe, von denen man in diesem Sommer schon einige Trauben ernten konnte, werden

auf das hinterste gut entwickelte Auge zurückgeschnitten. Der Schnitt wird ebenso in den folgenden Jahren gehandhabt. Wenn die Weinstöcke durch hohes Alter oder Krankheit Lücken in der Garnitur erhalten, so schneidet man einen möglichst tief stehenden starken Trieb, dem man keine Trauben gelassen hat, auf 0,5–1 m Länge und behandelt ihn, wie man vorher den alten Stock behandelt hatte, der nun abgeschnitten wird. Kurz vor Beginn des Treibens wird der Boden, soweit die Wurzeln reichen, mit einer 6 ctm starken Schicht frischen Kuh- oder Schweinemistes bedeckt. In jedem folgenden Jahr wird stets der alte Mist entfernt und durch frischen ersetzt. Ist nach einer Reihe von Jahren der Boden erschöpft oder haben einige Weinstöcke faule Wurzeln bekommen, so

wird die Erde theilweise erneuert, was auf folgende Weise geschieht: Die Hinterwand des Hauses entlang wird zunächst ein Graben von 1 Meter Tiefe und 0,75 m Breite mit möglichster Schonung der bis dahin vordringenden Wurzelspitzen gezogen, und die dabei gewonnene Erde aus dem Hause entfernt. Sodann wird mit Forken vorsichtig die Erde von der Vorderwand des Grabens losgelöst und zurückgeworfen, resp. hinausbefördert. Man schafft natürlich nur ein gleiches Quantum von alter Erde hinaus, wie man von neuer Erde hineinbringen will, die übrige Erde wird gegen die Rückwand des Hauses aufgehäuft. Die herausgelösten Wurzeln werden mit Häkchen auf der Erdoberfläche vor dem Graben befestigt, mit Wasser besprengt und mit Bastmatten bedeckt, damit

sie gegen Austrocknen geschützt sind. So wird mit der Arbeit fortgefahren, bis man die Weinstöcke vollständig, mit unverletzten Wurzeln herausgenommen hat. Nun wird die alte Erde mit der frischen gut gemischt und die Weinstöcke, nachdem die schlechten Wurzeln abgeschnitten sind, von neuem gepflanzt und zwar so, daß die Wurzeln gleichmäßig ausgebreitet sind und sich der Oberfläche nahe befinden. Der Boden wird schließlich mit einer 5–7 ctm hohen Schicht von kurzem Pferdemist bedeckt, welcher namentlich zu schnelles Austrocknen des Bodens an der Oberfläche verhindert. Diese Erderneuerung wird in England häufig und zwar wie mir sowohl *Mr. Harrison,* als auch andere tüchtige Weintreiber sagten, stets mit außerordentlichem Erfolge ausgeführt. Zum zweiten Treiben

S. 61

wird das Haus Fig. G (Nr. 10 des Planes [ ]) verwendet.

Um bei den im Hause vorzunehmenden Arbeiten das Festtreten der Erdoberfläche zu vermeiden, befinden sich in allen Häusern, wie in diesem, Läufer Fig. G, a, welche so angefertigt sind, wie Fig. D zeigt. Wo der Raum zum Anbringen von Läufern zu schmal ist, werden Bretter Fig. G, b hingelegt, um darauf treten zu können. Das Haus Nr. 10 ist, wie alle übrigen Häuser in *Knowsley* aus Holz construirt und zwar ist es, wie alle neueren daselbst, nicht mit beweglichen Fenstern bedeckt, sondern die Glasfläche wird durch stärkere und schwächere Sparren welche festliegen, getragen. Die Oberluftfenster e sind zusammenhängend gearbeitet. Durch diese Bauart spart man einerseits viel Geld andererseits ist dadurch das Haus

S. 62

viel fester geschlossen und hält sich so die Wärme darin viel besser, als in Häusern mit abnehmbaren Fenstern, natürlich auch viel besser, als in Häusern, welche aus Eisen erbaut sind. Die Häuser in *Knowsley* werden niemals zugedeckt trotzdem hält sich die Temperatur, selbst wenn draußen -17 bis -18°R sind, so gut, daß man, wenn die Feurungen Abends um 10 Uhr mit Kohlen gefüllt und die Thüren fest geschlossen sind, vor 6 Uhr Morgens nicht wieder nachzulegen braucht. Durch guten Anstrich halten sich die Häuser sehr lange. Die Heizungsvorrichtung entspricht der bei Figg. A und B angegeben; o in Figur G sind die Heißwasserröhren. Obgleich Röhren zur Bodenerwärmung vorhanden sind, werden dieselben nicht benutzt, da sich die Bodenheizung der Gesundheit der Weinstöcke gegenüber

S. 63

unvortheilhaft erwiesen hat. Durch die Vorrichtung d, deren unterer Theil Fig K, von vorn gesehen, zeigt, wird ein gleichmäßiges Öffnen des Luftfensters e in der Länge des ganzen Hauses ermöglicht, dasselbe geschieht durch die Vorrichtung f mit den unteren Luftfenstern.

Fig. I zeigt den Grundriß von der letzteren Vorrichtung; die Eisenstange i läuft durch das ganze Haus und öffnet, durch f in Umdrehung versetzt, sämmtliche Vorderfenster. Fig L ist der Grundriß des Hauses Nr. 10 mit der Heizröhrenleitung (o–o$^+$) die Röhren o^{IIII} und o$^+$ dienen zur Erwärmung des an das Weinhaus sich anschließenden Pfirsichhauses Nr. 11 des Planes. Zum zweiten Treiben werden außer den bereits vorher erwähnten Sorten: *Black Hamburgh*

S. 64

und *Foster's Seedling* noch folgende verwendet:
Madresfield Court, welche Sorte sich zum zweiten Treiben besser als zu jedem anderen zu eignen scheint. Die mittelgroßen, großbeerigen Trauben haben einen außerordentlich feinen Muscatgeschmack und eine schöne rothbraune Farbe, müssen aber sehr bald nach erlangter Reife gegessen werden, da sie sich leider nur kurze Zeit halten.
Royal Ascot mit kleinen, sehr großbeerigen, schwarzen Trauben,
Buckland Sweetwater, mit großen, großbeerigen, zart hellgelben Trauben, ist eine der besten Sorten zum zweiten Treiben, darf aber, wenn man vollkommene Trauben erlangen will, ebenso wie *Madresfield Court,* nicht zu kurz zugeschnitten werden.
Duke of Buccleuch, wovon sich in den *Knowlsey-Gardens* nur einige junge Stö-

S. 65

cke befanden, die zur Zeit meines dortseins noch nicht trugen, von *Mr. Harrison* und Anderen wurde diese Sorte wegen ihrer „schönen, festen, sehr großbeerigen, bernsteinfarbenen Trauben vom feinsten Aroma" sehr gelobt. Es sei hier erwähnt, daß man in England jedes Jahr dieselben Häuser in derselben Jahreszeit zum Treiben verwendet, dadurch wird den Stöcken stets eine gleiche Ruhezeit geboten. Will man den Stöcken nach einer besonders reichen Ernte mehr Ruhe gewähren, als sonst geschieht, so läßt man ihnen im nächsten Jahr nur eine mäßige Anzahl Trauben.
Nach erlangter Holzreife werden die Stöcke etwa Anfang October in vorbeschriebener Art geschnitten, sodann wird alle alte, lose Rinde abgeschabt, etwa vorhandene

S. 66

Löcher und Spalten mit flüssigem Baumwachs ausgefüllt, damit sich kein Ungeziefer darin einnistet, die Reben mit Bürsten gründlich gewaschen und zwar mit einer Auflösung von Seife und Salz in Tabackswasser. Darauf werden die Weinstöcke mit einem dickflüssigen Brei, bestehend aus Leimwasser mit Lehm, Schwefel, Tabackslauge, Seife und Soda angestrichen, um etwa noch zurückgebliebenes Ungeziefer zu tödten. Durch das Spritzen löst sich dieser Anstrich in Zeit von einigen Wochen wieder los von den Stämmen. Nachdem die Weinstöcke so vorbereitet, beginnt das Treiben um Mitte November. Die Erdoberfläche wird aufgelockert und, nach dem Gießen, mit Mist bedeckt. Da nämlich zur Erlangung einer guten Holzreife das Haus bis jetzt trocken gehalten wurde,

S. 67

so macht sich beim Beginn des Treibens ein tüchtiges Durchgießen des Bodens nöthig, das dazu benutzte Wasser muß eine Temperatur von circa 15°R haben. Das Durchgießen wiederholt sich, je nach Bedürfniß, alle 6–8 Wochen. Wasser, welches die erforderliche Temperatur hat, wird aus der Brauerei (Plan: k.) in einem großen Wasserwagen herbeigeschafft. Die fernere Behandlung ist der beim ersten Treiben angegebenen, analog, natürlich treten die einzelnen Perioden des Austreibens, Blühens, Reifens je etwa 14 Tage bis 3 Wochen später ein. Feuchte Luft wird durch Anfüllen der Bassins auf den Röhren mit Wasser und durch reichliches Spritzen erzeugt, ihr stetes Vorhandensein ist nicht nur zur Beförderung des Wachsthumsnöthig, son-

S. 68

dern auch zur Fernhaltung der gefährlichen rothen Spinne (*Acarus telarius*). Zeigt sich die letzere dennoch, so wird das Haus geschwefelt, indem dann die Heizungsröhren mit pulverisirtem, mit Wasser zu Brei gemengtem Schwefel bestrichen und sodann möglichst stark erhitzt werden. Hat man Weinsorten im Hause, deren Beeren eine zarte Haut haben, so darf man nicht zu stark schwefeln; Im Hause Nr. 5 wurde, als sich die Beeren zu färben begannen, stark geschwefelt, davon bekamen die Beeren von *Foster's Seedling* und *Bucklands Sweetwater* braune Streifen und wurden unansehnlich, *Black Hamburgh* dagegen blieb unberührt. Sobald die Beeren erbsengroß sind, beginnt das Ausbeeren und Auseinanderbinden der einzelnen Zweige der Trauben. Sobald sich die Beeren zu färben beginnen, also etwa

S. 69

um Mitte April, wird wiederum möglichst viel gelüftet. Nach der Ernte wird das Haus so trocken wie möglich gehalten. Die Temperatur beträgt in der ersten Woche des Treibens bei Tage 10° bei Nacht 6°R. steigt dann bis Ende Januar allmälig auf 13⁺° bei Tage und 10° bei Nacht, während des Februars steigt sie auf 16° bei Tage und 13° bei Nacht. In der Blüthezeit hält man das Haus auf 18° bei Tage und 10° bei Nacht. Nach der Blüthe läßt man die Temperatur wieder auf 14° bei Tage und 11° bei Nacht sinken.

Das Haus Nr 7–8 des Planes, früher aus 2 Abtheilungen bestehend, die jetzt vereinigt sind, wird Anfang Januar angetrieben, nachdem es ebenso vorbereitet ist, wie bei Nr. 10 beschrieben. Die Temperatur ist anfänglich auch dieselbe

S. 70

wie beim zweiten Treiben steigt in der Blüthezeit, also Mitte März, bis auf 19° bei Tage und 17° bei Nacht. Die zu diesem Treiben verwendeten Sorten sind:
Black Hamburgh,
Buckland Sweetwater,
Black Prince, mit großen schwarzen Trauben von gutem Geschmack, *Hamburgh Muscat,* dem *Black Hamburgh* ähnlich, jedoch von feinem Muscatgeschmack, trägt reichlich gute Trauben.
Zum vierten Treiben wird das Haus Nr. 5 des Planes verwendet. Das Treiben beginnt Mitte Februar, Vorbereitung und Methode des Treibens entsprechen ganz der vorbeschriebenen; ebenso ist es mit den später getriebenen Häusern. Alle Häuser werden am Beginn des Treibens bis zu erlangter Holzreife geheizt.
Zum viertem Treiben werden folgende Sorten verwendet:

S. 71

Ferdinand de Lesseps, mit kleiner, weißer Traube, reichtragend,
Foster's Seedling
Buckland Sweetwater
Black Hamburg, in einer sehr schönen Varietät mit sehr dunklen, großen Beeren.
Das Haus Nr 6 wird zum nächsten Treiben, Beginn: Mitte März, verwendet, die darin befindlichen Sorten sind:
Madresfield Court, fing gleich nach der Reife an zu faulen, ebenso
Golden Champin[5] *[sic]* mit sehr großbeeriger, großer schön dunkelgelber Traube von außerordentlichem Wohlgeschmack, leider wird jedoch das Holz nur in besonders günstigen Jahren zur Noth reif;
Child of Hale, wurde durch den berühmten Weintreiber *Meredith* in *Garston* aus Samen gezogen, unterscheidet sich durchaus nicht von *Trebbiano,* einer Sorte mit schöner großer Traube

S. 72

von weißer Farbe und sehr fadem Geschmack.
Mrs. Pince, große Traube mit mittelgroßen, dunkelrothen Beeren von feinem Muscatgeschmack.
Raisin de Calabre, sehr große weiße Traube, Geschmack nicht gut,

5 Jancke likely meant "champion."

Black Alicante, eine der empfehlenswerthesten Sorten zum Spättreiben, Trauben groß, großbeerig, schwarz, fein beduftet, sehr wohlschmeckend, halten sich sehr lange nach der Reife.

Lady Downe's Seedling, mit kleinen, sehr großbeerigen Trauben, Farbe schwarz, Geschmack gut, ebenfalls sehr empfehlenswerth.

Die Häuser Nr 1, 2, 3, 4 und 9 werden Anfang April angetrieben.

In Nr 1 befindet sich nur *Muscat of Alexandria,* ein vorzüglicher, hellgelber, sehr süßer Muscatwein von unübertrefflichem Aroma, die Trauben halten sich so lange wie keine andere

S. 73

Sorte. Die Mäuse stellen allen Muscatweinen sehr nach, deshalb deckt man über jede Traube ein Stück Matte, mit der rauhen Seite nach oben gekehrt. Die Mäuse lieben es nicht, die Matte mit den Pfoten zu berühren und die Trauben bleiben verschont.

In Nr 2 befindet sich außer *Muscat of Alexandria* noch ein junger Stock von *Dr. Hogg,* dies soll eine sehr gute, weiße Sorte mit Muscatgeschmack sein.

In Nr 3 befinden sich:

Black Hamburgh, welcher, auf *Lady Downe's* veredelt, sehr gut trägt,

Barbarossa, eine sehr späte, schwarze Sorte mit außerordentlich großen Trauben.

In Nr 4 sind folgende Sorten angepflanzt:

Black Hamburgh,

Champion Muscat, auf *Black Hamburgh* veredelt, mit schöner, rother

S. 74

Traube. Dieselbe Sorte, auf *Muscat of Alexandria* veredelt, trägt noch besser, auch *Duke of Buccleuch* soll, auf *Muscat of Alexandria* veredelt, besonders gute Erträge liefern. Ferner:

Muscat Hamburgh

Madresfield Court

Duke of Buccleuch.

Alle Häuser lieferten im Jahr 74 einen sehr reichen Ertrag von so großen und schönen Trauben, wie ich sie auf dem Continet noch nicht gesehen hatte.

Nicht minder gute Resultate wurden in der Pfirsichtreiberei erzielt.

Man bedient sich zu derselben der Häuser Nr 11 & 12 des Planes und zwar wird Nr 12, Fig M zuerst angetrieben. Beide Häuser sind im Allgemeinen ebenso construirt, wie das Weinhaus Fig. G. Der Aufriß des Hauses ist in Fig. H dargestellt, ein Theil des Grundrisses in Fig L rechts. An jedem

stärkeren Sparren des Hauses ist ein eiserner Bügel, Fig M, a durch die Eisen
b befestigt. Durch diesen Bügel laufen die etwa 5 Millimeter starken Drähte,
welche von einander 13 Centimeter entfernt sind, und zum Anhaften der
Bäume dienen. Dies eiserne Spalier nähert sich der Glasfläche nur bis auf
0,5 Meter, durch diese Entfernung sind die Bäume dem nachtheiligen Einfluß
des Wetters entzogen im Sommer sind sie gegen Verbrennen, im Winter gegen
Erkältung mehr geschützt, als dies bei Spalieren der Fall ist, welche sich der
Glasfläche zu nahe befinden.
An der Hinterwand ist gleichfalls ein Drahtspalier zur Anhaftung von
Pfirsichbäumen, diese liefern ebenfalls einen guten Ertrag. Die Pfirsichbäume
sind in Fächerform gezogen, welche für sie die

natürlichste und am leichtesten zu erziehende ist. Das ganze Spalier ist
gleichmäßig mit jungem Holz bedeckt und zur Reifezeit ebenso gleichmäßig
mit Früchten. Die älteren Zweige sind, wie die jüngeren, gerade, glatt
und gesund. Der Schnitt beschränkt sich darauf, im Herbst Zweige da zu
entfernen, wo sie zu dicht stehen. Sobald sich im Sommer die Endknospen
ausgebildet haben, das Holzwachsthum also aufgehört hat, werden die Triebe
auf 15–20 ctm. pincirt und die Wassertriebe entfernt, letztere Manipulation
wird öfter wiederholt.
Die Vorbereitungen zum Frühtreiben beginnen Mitte October. Die Bäume
werden, nachdem sie geschnitten sind, sorgfältig gereinigt. Wenn weiße
Läuse an den jüngsten Zweigen vorhanden sind werden dieselben mittelst
eines Borstenpinsels und Spiritus

gereinigt. Die älteren Zweige werden mit den bei der Weintreiberei
beschriebenen Mischungen gereinigt und angestrichen. Sobald der Anstrich
getrocknet ist, werden die Bäume mit Bast sorgfältig so angebunden, daß das
Spalier ganz gleichmäßig bedeckt ist und alle Zweige von einander gleichen
Abstand haben. In der ersten Hälfte des November wird die Oberfläche des
Erdbodens aufgelockert, das Haus gründlich gewässert und der Boden 8
Centimeter hoch mit Kuhmist bedeckt. Das Haus, welches bis jetzt reichlich Luft erhalten hatte, wird nun geschlossen und Mitte November mit dem
Treiben begonnen. Die Temperatur beträgt in der ersten Woche bei Tage 8°,
bei Nacht 5°R und wird bis zur Blüthezeit, welche um Mitte Januar eintritt,
bis auf 11° bei Tage und 9° bei

S. 78

Nacht gesteigert. Kurz vor der Blüthe wird der Boden noch einmal tüchtig durchgegossen, weil die Blüthen leicht abfallen, wenn der Boden zu trocken ist. Von Beginn des Treibens an bis zum Aufbrechen der Blüthen werden die Bäume täglich 2 Mal, gewöhnlich Morgens um 9 und Nachmittags um 2 Uhr mit lauwarmen Wasser so gespritzt, daß keine trockne Stelle am Baum bleibt. Während der Blüthezeit wird eine gleichmäßige Feuchtigkeit durch öfteres leichtes Bespritzen des Bodens erhalten. Ein Bespritzen der Blüthen hat zur Folge, daß durch die Berührung mit dem Wasser die Pollenkörnchen durch Endosmose so schnell anschwellen, daß die Pollenschläuche platzen und ihren Inhalt auf die Narbe fließen lassen, anstatt durch das Pistill zum Ovarium zu dringen. Um eine recht allgemeine Be-

S. 79

fruchtung zu erzielen, erzeugt man außer reichlicher Lüftung mittelst der Luftfenster, mit einem an einen Stock gebundenen Gänseflügel einen künstlichen Luftzug, außerdem erhöht man bis zu Ende der Blüthezeit die Temperatur nicht, um so die Dauer derselben zu verlängern und den Blüthen möglichst viel Zeit zur Befruchtung zu lassen.

Nach der Blüthe bis zur Steinbildung, welche sich durch einen Stillstand im Wachsthum der Früchte anzeigt, erhöht man die Temperatur allmälig auf 13–14° bei Tage und 12° bei Nacht. Das Spritzen wird wiederum auf die Bäume ausgedehnt. Während der Steinbildung wird dieselbe Temperatur beibehalten. Es werden nun so viele Früchte ausgebrochen, daß nur auf jedem Quadrat-

S. 80

Meter der von Baum bedeckten Fläche etwa 10 Früchte sitzen bleiben, welche möglichst gleichmäßig über die ganze Fläche vertheilt sind.

Nach der Steinbildung wird wiederum gegossen. Mit dem Eintreten höherer Wärme muß gleichzeitig das Spritzen häufiger wiederholt werden, da sich bei zu trockener Luft sofort die grüne Laus einstellt. Findet sie sich trotz aller Vorsicht doch an, so wird das Haus mit Tabackspapier geräuchert; der Taback selbst ist in England zu theuer, um zu diesem Zweck benutzt zu werden.

Nach der Steinbildung bis zu der Zeit, zu welcher sich die Früchte zu färben beginnen, erhöht man die Temperatur nach und nach auf 18° bei Tage und 16° bei Nacht. Sobald sich die Früchte zu färben beginnen wird das Bespritzen der Bäume selbst ein-

S. 81

gestellt. Während der Reifezeit, welche um Mitte Mai eintritt, behält man die-selbe Temperatur bei, lüftet aber sehr reichlich und schließt auch bei Nacht die

Luftfenster nicht ganz, da stetiger frischer Luftzug den Geschmack der Früchte außerordentlich verbessert. Die Ernte im Mai 74 war eine sehr gute zu nennen. Das Gießen erfolgt je nach Bedürfniß; in *Knowsley* werden die Pfirchsichhäuser während des ganzen Jahres 4–5 Mal gewässert. Zu dem Frühtreiben werden folgende Sorten benutzt:

1. Pfirsich:

Royal George (Madeleine à petites fleurs) trug sehr reichlich schöne, saftige und wohlschmeckende Früchte und ist jedenfalls eine der besten Sorten zum Frühtreiben,

Bellegarde reifte als zweite, gleichfalls eine vorzügliche Treibsorte von gro-

S. 82

ßem Wohlgeschmack, mit kleinen Blüthen und großen Früchten, hält sich nach dem Abpflücken länger, als die meisten anderen,

Violette hâtive, ebenfalls gut zum Treiben mit großen, schönen und guten Früchten,

Barrington, stellt sich den drei vorgenannten ebenbürtig an die Seite, sowohl in Bezug auf Tragbarkeit, als auch auf Wohlgeschmack der Früchte. Außerdem befindet sich im Haus ein junger Baum von *Dagmar,* welche Sorte auch zum Treiben sehr empfohlen wird.

2. Nectarinen:

Hunts' Tanny wurde von den Nectarinen zuerst reif, trägt reichlich Früchte mit vom Stein sich ablösendem Fleisch, wird bald nach eingetretener Reife mehlig, muß daher bald verbraucht werden.

S. 83

Elruge, gleichfalls mit ablösendem Fleisch, ist eine der besten Nectarinen und eignet sich vorzüglich zum Treiben,

Violette hâtive, ebenfalls in jeder Hinsicht sehr empfehlenswerth zum Treiben, mit ablösendem Fleisch,

Impératrice, ablösend, gut, wohlschmeckend, sehr gut zum Treiben.

Zum zweiten Pfirsichtreiben wird Haus Nr 11 des Planes verwendet, welches ebenso construirt ist wie Nr 12 (Fig. M). Das zweite Treiben beginnt nach der beim ersten Treiben schon beschriebenen Vorbereitung, welche hier im Dezember vollendet wird, um Mitte Januar. Die Behandlung ist im allgemeinen dieselbe wie beim ersten Treiben. Die Blüthezeit tritt Anfang Februar ein, die Fruchtreife im Juni. Die zum zweiten

S. 84

Treiben verwendeten Sorten sind folgende:
Royal George

Bellegarde

Violette hâtive

Barrington

Diese vier empfehlen sich zum zweiten Treiben ebenso, wie zum ersten.

Grosse Mignonne, sehr gut zum Treiben, trägt reichlich große schöne und sehr wohlschmeckende Früchte,

Noblesse trägt zahlreiche, sehr große, blasse Früchte, die an Wohlgeschmack wohl alle anderen Sorten übertreffen.

Von Nectarinen befinden sich im Hause:

Elruge

Violette hâtive

Impératrice, welche auch beim zweiten Treiben einen reichen und guten Ertrag lieferten.

Zur <u>Feigentreiberei</u> wird das Haus Nr 25 des Planes benutzt; Figur N zeigt einen Durchschnitt, Figur

S. 85

O, 2 den Grundriß desselben (Fig O, 1 ist der Grundriß des Kirschhauses). Durch 2 Hebel, Fig N, k, welche sich an beiden Enden des Hauses befinden, werden die Vorderfenster geöffnet, ebenso werden die Oberfenster durch 2 Hebelvorrichtungen geöffnet. Vorn im Hause stehen 2 Reihen Feigenbäume. Die mit Spalier versehene Hinterwand wird durch 2 fächerförmig gezogene Feigenbäume fast ganz bedeckt.

Den Sommer über erhalten die Feigenbäume reichlich Wasser. Zu schwache Triebe werden fortgeschnitten. Die Früchte, welche sich bis Ende Juli bilden, werden fortgebrochen, da sie sich doch nicht gut entwickeln würden, die später sich zeigenden läßt man an dem Baum sitzen, sie sind die zuerst reifenden.

S. 86

Die Vorbereitungen zum Treiben beginnen im Dezember. Strohige Überbleibsel von der vorjährigen Dungschicht werden entfernt, die Bäume von der sich jährlich einstellenden weißen Laus (*Coccus adonidum L.*) mit Borstenpinsel und Spiritus entfernt und dann mittelst scharfer Bürsten mit Tabackslauge, worin Seife und Soda aufgelöst isind [*sic*], gewaschen. Nachdem dies geschehen ist, werden sorgfältig alle Löcher und Ritzen im alten Stamm mit *Mastic L`homme Lefort* zugeklebt da dieselben stets dem Ungeziefer als Brutstätten dienen. So dann werden die ganzen Bäume, mit Ausnahme der jüngsten Triebe, mit dem schon früher beschriebenen Brei bestrichen. Nachdem der Anstrich völlig angetrocknet ist, werden die Zweige der Bäume, welche dem Glas zu nahe kommen, mit starkem Bind-

faden heruntergebunden, so daß manche Bäume fast den Eindruck von
Trauerbäumen machen; dies Herunterbiegen soll auch zugleich den
Fruchtansatz begünstigen, die zu dicht an einander stehenden Zweige
werden durch Bindfaden aus einander gebunden, so daß alle Zweige der
Krone möglichst gleichen Abstand von einander haben.

In der ersten Hälfte des Januar wird die Erdoberfläche im Feigenhaus
aufgelockert, und zwar ganz leicht und vorsichtig, um die Wurzeln der
Feigenbäume nicht zu verletzen, welche zum großen Theil ganz dicht unter
der Oberfläche liegen. Der Erdboden wird jetzt noch einmal ganz gründlich
durchgegossen und darauf mit einer 5–7 ctm hohen Lage festen Kuhmistes

bedeckt, worauf das Treiben beginnt.

Die Temperatur des Hauses wird nun zuerst auf 9° bei Tage und 7° bei Nacht
gehalten, die Wasserbehälter auf den Heizungsröhren stets mit Wasser
gefüllt erhalten, und die Bäume täglich 2 Mal Morgens und Nachmittags, mit
lauwarmen Wasser von allen Seiten überspritzt. Die Temperatur des Hauses
wird allmälig bis Ende März auf 16° bei Tage und 14° bei Nacht gesteigert und
das Spritzen mit der Wärmezunahme täglich öfter wiederholt. Soweit die
Witterung es irgend erlaubt, wird Luft gegeben, da nur bei reichlicher Lüftung
wohlschmeckende Früchte erzielt werden.

Bei Sonnenschein spritzt man jetzt die Blätter nicht mehr, da sie sonst leicht
schlecht werden, sondern nur noch den Boden

und die Stämme. Das Gießen muß von Zeit zu Zeit wiederholt werden, da die
Feigenbäume in ihrer Wachstumsperiode viel Wasser verlangen. Von April an
wird dem Boden nicht mehr zu viel Feuchtigkeit zugeführt, da ein Übermaß
derselben den Früchten, welche sich der Reifezeit nähern, einen wässrigen
Geschmack giebt und außerdem oft bewirkt, daß dieselben aufplatzen, dessen
ungeachtet darf man aber die Luft nicht zu trocken werden lassen, sondern
durch öfteres leichtes Überspritzen des Bodens die nöthige Feuchtigkeit
erhalten.

Von April bis zur Reifezeit, welche Anfang Mai eintritt, wird die Temperatur
weiter auf 17° bei Tage und 15° bei Nacht erhöht, bei Sonnenschein kann sie,
wie bei jedem Treiben

5° höher steigen, bei trübem und kaltem Wetter 2–3° geringer sein. Mitte Juni
wird eine zweite Ernte gehalten. Nach der Ernte wird so viel wie möglich

gelüftet und reichlich gegossen. Die in *Knowsley* zum Treiben verwendeten Sorten sind folgende:

Brown Turkey ist eine der am meisten zum Treiben geeigneten Sorten und liefert einen enormen Ertrag von schön gefärbten, äußerst wohlschmeckenden Früchten,

White Marseilles, gleichfalls gut zum Treiben, frühreifend, sehr süß,

Carte Kennedy, mit großer, sehr süßer Frucht, brachte einen sehr guten Ertrag.

Das Haus welches zur <u>Kirschentreiberei</u> benutzt wird, ist ebenso gebaut, wie das Feigenhaus, hat jedoch nicht soviele Heizröhren, da die Kirschen

S. 91

nicht einer so intensiven Wärme bedürfen, wie die Feigen. Während auf jedes Kubikmeter Inhalt des Kirschhauses nur etwa 8,3 Quadratdecimeter Heizröhrenoberfläche kommen, sind im Feigenhaus auf jedes Kubikmeter 14,7 Quadratdecimeter gerechnet.

Der Grundriß des Kirschhauses mit den Röhren ist in Fig. O, 1 dargestellt. Der Durchschnitt ist wie der des Feigenhauses nur fallen 2 Röhren fort, und in dem Raum vor dem Wege stehen, statt zweier, drei Reihen Bäume.

An der Hinterwand stehen fächerförmig gezogene Kirschenbäume und zwar folgende Sorten:

Transparent, sehr schmackhaft mit durchsichtiger Haut, trägt nicht sehr reich,

Black Tartarian trägt gute, große, schwarze Früchte in großer Anzahl,

S. 92

Bigarreau, weiß, sehr wohlschmeckend, reichtragend.

In dem vorderen Theil des Hauses stehen:

May duke, die beste zum Treiben, trägt sehr dankbar

Black Eagle, sehr wohlschmeckend,

Reine Hortense, bringt große, rothe Früchte, doch nicht sehr zahlreich.

Nachdem man den Kirschbäumen den Sommer und Herbst über soviel Luft wie möglich gewährt und sie öfter gegossen hat, hin und wieder auch mit Dungwasser, wird Ende December die Erdoberfläche aufgelockert, doch sehr vorsichtig, da die Wurzeln ebenso flach liegen wie bei den Feigen. Nach einem tüchtigen Durchgießen wird nun der Erdboden mit Kuhmist bedeckt. Gewaschen oder angestrichen wurden die Kirschbäume nicht, da sich kein Ungeziefer an denselben zeigte. Mit dem Treiben beginnt man erst

S. 93

Anfang Januar, da ein früheres Treiben, bei der Seltenheit des Sonnenscheins Ende Winters, einen guten Fruchtansatz zu sehr in Frage stellt.

Die Temperatur beträgt anfänglich bei Tage 8° bei Nacht 4°R. Die Bäume werden nun täglich, je nach der Witterung 1–2 Mal tüchtig mit lauwarmem Wasser gespritzt und, so weit es die Witterung erlaubt, wird reichlich gelüftet.

Bis zur Blüthezeit, welche in der ersten Hälfte des Februar eintritt, wird die Temperatur auf 10° bei Tage und 8° bei Nacht erhöht. Eine künstliche Befruchtung wird nicht vorgenommen.

Das Spritzen der Bäume wird während der Blüthezeit eingestellt, doch wird die nöthige Feuchtigkeit durch Sprengen des Bodens erhalten. In der Blüthezeit muß man namentlich den

S. 94

Bäumen soviel frische Luft, wie möglich, zu kommen lassen. Nach dem Abblühen werden wiederum die ganzen Bäume gespritzt und die Temperatur wird bis zur Reife allmälig auf 15° bei Tage und 12° bei Nacht erhöht. Während der Zeit der Steinbildung werden die jungen Zweige der Bäume nicht gespritzt, auch erhalten die Bäume in dieser Zeit keinen Guß. Sobald die Früchte anfangen sich zu färben, werden die Bäume nicht mehr gespritzt und über die Luftfenster wird ein Netz gezogen, um den Sperlingen das Eindringen unmöglich zu machen. (Auch die Kirschen, welche an den Mauern des Küchengartens stehen, werden, sobald sie sich zu färben beginnen, mit Netzen überzogen).

Die Reife tritt im April ein. Der Ertrag war im Jahr 74 verhältnißmäßig gut.

S. 95

Für die Ananastreiberei ist in *Knowsley* ein Haus erbaut, welches aus 2 Abtheilungen besteht, Fig. P ist ein Durchschnitt, Fig. R der Grundriß davon, Fig. Q der Aufriß eines Theiles des Hauses.

Fig S ist der Aufriß der Röhre a in Fig R, die Röhre b ist ebenso eingerichtet, bei c und d fehlen die Schieber e, e durch welche man bei a und b das heiße Wasser von der kälteren Abtheilung, je nach Bedürfniß, absperren kann.

Junge Ananaspflanzen werden aus den alten gewonnen, nachdem die letzteren Frucht getragen haben, indem man den kräftigsten der zwischen den Blättern sich entwickelnden Triebe wachsen läßt, die übrigen aber abschneidet, den oberhalb des Triebes befindlichen Theil der alten Pflanze gleichfalls

S. 96

fortnimmt und die Wunden mit Kohlenpulver bestreut, um Fäulniß zu verhüten. Die alten Pflanzen bleiben bis zum Februar im Hause stehen und werden während des Winters trocken gehalten. Ende Februar wird für die jungen Pflanzen der Kasten hinter dem Ananashause mit Mist und Laub angelegt, und zwar so, daß nach dem Sinken des Mistes dessen Oberfläche 0,6 Meter von dem Glas entfernt ist. Der Kasten ist etwa 2 Meter tief. Die jungen Triebe oder Kindel werden zu gleicher Zeit von der Mutterpflanze abgenommen, von den unteren Blättern behutsam befreit und in 16 Centimeter weite Töpfe gepflanzt in eine Mischung von lehmiger Rasenerde mit geringen [sic] Zusatz von stückiger Heideerde und Sand. Nachdem die Temperatur des

S. 97

Mistes bis auf 22°R gesunken ist, also etwa 14 Tage nach der Anlage des Beetes, wird der Mist mit einer 2–3^{dcm} hohen Schicht Lohe bedeckt und die Kindel so dahineingefüttert, daß sie 0,5 Meter Abstand von einander haben.

Unmittelbar nach dem Einpflanzen werden die Kindel leicht angegossen, darauf erhalten sie nicht eher wieder einen Guß, als bis sich die Wurzeln zu entwickeln anfangen, was man leicht daran erkennt, daß sich neue Blätter im Herzen entwickeln. Sodann wird mit lauwarmem Wasser alle 3–5 Tage, je nach Bedürfniß, gegossen. In den ersten Wochen nach dem Einbringen der Pflanzen wird der Kasten nur sehr wenig gelüftet und zwar nur, um die aus dem Mist sich entwickelnden Dämpfe entweichen

S. 98

zu lassen. So lange Nachtfröste zu befürchten sind, wird das Beet bei Nacht mit Strohdecken zugedeckt. Während des Sommers wird täglich, aber auch nur in geringem Maße, gelüftet, und bei großer Hitze leicht beschattet, auch werden die Pflanzen täglich mit lauwarmem Wasser überspritzt. Von Zeit zu Zeit wird dem Wasser zum Begießen Dungwasser (aus Hirschmist bereitet) zugemischt. Im November werden die jungen Pflanzen in die mit Laub gefüllten Beete der kälteren Abtheilung des Ananashauses bis zur Hälfte ihrer Höhe eingefüttert; den Winter über werden die Pflanzen nicht zu naß gehalten.

Die Temperatur beträgt anfänglich bei Tage 13° bei Nacht 10°R und wird bis zum Mai all-

S. 99

mälig auf 18° bei Tage und 15° bei Nacht erhöht.

Vom Februar an beginnt man die Pflanzen wiederum zu bespritzen und durch Gießen der Wände und Wege feuchte Luft zu erzeugen. Anfang Mai werden die jungen Pflanzen in 25–30 ctm weite Töpfe gepflanzt und zwar in dieselbe Mischung wie vorher. Den Sommer über wird das Haus sehr reichlich gelüftet und gespritzt, die Pflanzen mit Dungwasser gegossen und die Temperatur bis zum Juli auf 21° bei Tage und 18° bei Nacht gesteigert.

(Den nächsten Winter geht man mit der Temperatur wieder auf 12–13°
herunter und hält die Pflanzen sehr trocken).
Im September werden die im Sommer kräftig herangewachsenen
Ananaspflanzen wiederum

S. 100

in etwas größere Töpfe verpflanzt und in die frisch angelegten Laubbeete der
warmen Abtheilung gebracht, so, daß sie alle reichlich Platz haben (etwa 1 m
von einander entfernt). Die Pflanzen erhalten ein einmaliges Angießen und
werden nun bis zum Januar vollständig trocken gehalten. Die Temperatur
beträgt in dieser ganzen Zeit bei Tage 13, bei Nacht 10°R. Die Luft wird
trocken gehalten und durch die Luftvorrichtungen vorsichtig erneuert.
Nachdem die Pflanzen so einige Monate geruht, fängt man Ende Januar an, sie
zu treiben; sie werden mit lauwarmem Wasser angegossen und die Temperatur
erhöht. Sobald die Pflanzen anfangen neue Blätter zu machen und die alten
Blätter sich ausbreiten,

S. 101

fängt man wiederum an, sie mit lauwarmem Wasser zu überspritzen. Während
der Blüthezeit wird das Spritzen eingestellt. Nach dem Abblühen fängt man
sogleich wieder an, reichlich zu spritzen und häufig mit Wasser von 20–30°R
zu gießen, etwa 1 Mal wöchentlich wird Dungwasser angewendet.
Die Temperatur wird bis zur Reifezeit auf 22° bei Tage und 20° bei Nacht
erhöht.
Sobald die Früchte sich der Reife nähern, wird das Gießen vermindert. Die
Pflanzen waren in *Knowsley* im vorigen Jahr sehr gesund und, mit Ausnahme
von vieren, ganz frei von Ungeziefer. Diese besagten 4 Pflanzen wurden,
sobald sich an ihnen die Schildträger (*Coccus bromeliae*) zeigten, aus dem
Hause entfernt und brachten in

S. 102

einem Mistbeet ihre Früchte zur Reife.
Die in *Knowsley* cultivirten Sorten sind folgende:
Black Jamaica, mit dunkelbraungrüner Frucht, welche erst bei Eintritt der
Reife eine hellere, gelbe Farbe annimmt, sie wird als eine der dankbarsten
und wohlschmeckendsten bezeichnet, Frucht eiförmig;
Smooth leaved Cayenne hat stachellose Blätter und große Früchte, die oben
so breit wie unten sind, soll gleichfalls ein gutes Aroma haben, außer diesen
Montserrat, ferner verschiedene Varietäten von *Queen,* die ebenfalls
empfehlenswerth sind,
White Providence, mit großer, aber nicht feiner Frucht.

Zur <u>Melonentreiberei</u> werden in *Knowsley* folgende Sorten verwendet: *Malvern Hall* ist eine der besten zum Treiben,

S. 103

die Frucht ist gerippt, das Fleisch roth,
Victory of Bath, mit länglich elliptischer Frucht, wird abgeschnitten bevor sie volle Reife erlangt hat,
Colston Basset, gleichfalls eine gute Treibsorte mit gerippter Frucht und weißem Fleisch,
Trentham hybrid, eine sehr empfehlenswerthe, leicht gerippte Netzmelone von länglicher Form und hellgelbem Fleisch, trägt sehr früh und wird sowohl im Hause, als auch im Freien cultivirt.
Dr. Hogg, mit dickschaliger, rein gelber gerippter, fast kugelrunder Frucht,
Conqueror ist die frühste Netzmelone mit großer, 3–4 lb. schwerer, gerippter Frucht,
Incomparable ist eine sehr gute, gerippte Netzmelone mit grünem Fleisch.

S. 104

Zum Treiben wird das Haus Nr 13 des Planes benutzt, welches ähnlich wie das Gurkenhaus (Fig. A) eingerichtet, doch bedeutend kleiner ist.
Außerdem werden auf dem Culturstück hinter dem Küchengarten Melonen gezogen und zwar nach der in Frankreich sehr gebräuchlichen Glockenculturmethode.
Zum Zweck des Treibens werden Anfang Januar die ersten Melonen in Töpfe gesät, welche im Weinhaus Nr 23 des Planes Unterkommen finden. Man bedient sich zur ersten Anzucht der Sorte *Conqueror.*
Sobald die Töpfe in das Weinhaus gestellt sind, werden sie mit einem Drahtgeflecht umgeben und bedeckt, um die Mäuse und Schnecken davon fern zu halten. Sobald die Töpfe voll Wurzeln sind und die

S. 105

Pflanzen 3–4 Blätter gemacht haben, was Mitte Februar der Fall ist, werden sie in die für sie vorbereiteten Beete des Melonenhauses gepflanzt. Die Vorbereitung besteht darin, daß man im Januar die Beete mit Laub und Mist füllt und fest antritt, nach etwa 14 Tagen bringt man hierauf eine 5 Centimeter hohe Lage von Lehm, mit halb verrottetem Mist gemengt. Unter der Mitte eines jeden Fensters wird ein Haufen von derselben Mischung, etwa 15 Centimeter hoch und 30 Centimeter breit, aufgeschüttet und dahinein je eine Pflanze gepflanzt. Man überbraust nun den Hügel öfters mit lauwarmem Wasser, 2 Mal wöchentlich wird ein Dungguß gegeben. Sobald die Wurzeln den Hügel durch-wachsen haben und sich an dessen Außenseiten die Spitzen zeigen, wird derselbe mit einer neuen Schicht von derselben Mischung umgeben und so fortgefahren, bis das Beet ziemlich gleichmäßig damit angefüllt ist.

Die Temperatur des Hauses beträgt in der ersten Woche des Treibens bei Tage 17° bei Nacht 15°R, und wird bis zur Reife, welche Mitte Mai eintritt, allmälig auf 20° bei Tage und 18° bei Nacht gesteigert. Sobald die Pflanzen 6–7 Blätter gemacht haben, werden sie abgestutzt, so daß jede nun 2 Ranken bildet, welche an je einem Stabe bis zu dem 20 Centimeter von der Glasfläche entfernten Spalier geleitet werden.

Luft wird vom Beginn des Treibens an täglich, je nach Maßgabe der Witterung, stärker oder

schwächer gegeben und zwar nach der Reifezeit hin immer reichlicher. Sobald die Pflanzen in Blüthe sind, wird mit einem feinen Pinsel der Pollen von den männlichen auf die Pistille der weiblichen Blüthen übertragen. Sobald die Früchte größer werden, legt man sie auf Brettchen, welche mit einem Ende auf einem Spalierdraht liegen und deren anderes Ende mittelst Bindfaden an dem nächsthöheren Draht befestigt ist.

Die Cultur bei den später gesäten Sorten ist im Allgemeinen dieselbe.

Zur Cultur im Freien wird *Trentham hybrid* benutzt. Man wirft zu derselben einen meterhohen Wall auf, der sich nach Süden sanft abdacht. Auf diesen Wall werden, nachdem er 5 ctm

hoch mit kurzem halb verrottetem Pferdemist bedeckt ist, die jungen Pflanzen im April, wenn sie 3–4 Blätter gemacht haben, so gepflanzt, daß sie einen Meter von einander entfernt sind, so dann werden sie mit Glasglocken bedeckt, welche in kühlen Nächten mit alten Bastmatten gedeckt werden. Die Glocken werden durch Unterlagen von Hölzern nach und nach mehr gelüftet und zuletzt ganz fortgenommen, so daß sich die Pflanzen auf dem Südabhang ausbreiten können. Die Behandlung derselben ist ähnlich wie die im Hause.

In Frankreich legt man die Wälle von Norden nach Süden laufend an und läßt von den 2 Ranken einer Pflanze je eine auf dem Ost- die andere auf dem Westabhange liegen.

Zur Gurkentreiberei wird das Haus Nr 22 des Planes benutzt, von welchem Fig. A 1 den Durchschnitt, Figur B den Grundriß zeigt.

Zum Treiben wurde in *Knowsley* im vorigen Jahr ausschließlich *Rollisons Telegraph* als eine der besten Treibgurken verwendet. Die Früchte werden 50–60 Centimeter lang, bleiben fast ganz gerade und haben einen feinen Geschmack. Die Aussaat geschieht in der zweiten Hälfte des August in Töpfe, welche in einem Mistbeet Aufstellung finden.

Anfang October, wenn die Pflanzen 3–4 Blätter gemacht haben, werden sie in das Gurkenhaus gebracht. Die Beete sind schon einige Wochen vorher mit Laub und Mist gefüllt und, nachdem die Tem-

S. 110

peratur derselben angefangen hat zu sinken, mit einer 20 Centimeter hohen Schicht von Erde bedeckt worden; die Mischung besteht aus Lehm, Lauberde und verrottetem Pferdemist aus alten Champignonbeeten.

Anfang October wird die Erde so zusammen gescharrt, daß die Haufen 1,5 m von einander entfernt sind. In diese Haufen wird je eine Gurke gepflanzt, und, sobald die Wurzeln sich weiter ausdehnen, werden die Haufen mit Erde von derselben Mischung umkleidet.

In der Blüthezeit nimmt man Mittags die Befruchtung mit einem Pinsel vor. Die Temperatur des Hauses wird ziemlich gleichmäßig auf 20°R bei Tage und 17° bei Nacht gehalten und die Pflanzen ziemlich reichlich, namentlich, wenn die Früch-

S. 111

te schwellen, gegossen. Die ersten Früchte werden im Dezember, die letzten im Mai geerntet. Nach der Ernte werden die Pflanzen entfernt, das Beet frisch angelegt und mit neuen Gurken bepflanzt.

Für die <u>Bohnenzucht</u> ist in *Knowsley* kein besonderes Haus eingerichtet, sondern man benutzt zu ihrer Aufstellung die Ränder der Beete und das Fensterbrett im Ananashause, die Kästen hinter demselben Hause, so lange sie disponibel sind und das Melonenhaus. Die zum Treiben benutzten Bohnen sind: *Williams's* und *Osborne's,* beide sehr niedrig bleibend und einen reichen Ertrag von allerdings ziemlich kleinen Früchten liefernd. Zum Anschluß an die Ernte von den im Freien, auf dem

S. 112

Beet vor den Häusern Nr 10 bis 12 stehenden Bohnen wird Anfang September eine Aussaat in ein halb kaltes Mistbeet gemacht, und darauf alle 14 Tage eine Aussaat in Töpfe von 25 ctm Durchmesser gemacht. Die Töpfe werden bis zur Hälfte mit lockerer Mistbeeterde gefüllt und legt man dahinein 10 Bohnen im Kreise, etwa 5 Centimeter von Rande entfernt und 4 ctm tief. Diese Töpfe

werden in das Melonenhaus gestellt, woselbst die Temperatur von November
bis Januar auf 16° bei Tage und 14° bei Nacht gehalten wird; gegossen wird wenig.
Sobald die Pflanzen einige Blätter gemacht haben, werden die Töpfe bis auf
⅔ ihrer Höhe mit Mistbeeterde nachgefüllt und nach dem Ananashause
hinüberbefördert, wo sie auf den seitlichen Fen-

S. 113

sterbrettern und den Rändern der aus rothen Sandsteinplatten zusammen-
gefügten Beete Platz finden. Durch Einstecken von Besenreisern wird den
Pflanzen ein Halt gegeben.
Die jüngste Aussaat wird jedes Mal an die wärmste Stelle des Melonenhauses
gestellt. Die Ernte erfolgt etwa 2 Monate nach der Aussaat.
Im Januar, wenn das Melonenhaus zur Aufnahme der Melonen vorbereitet wird,
bereitet man ein Mistbeet für die folgenden Bohnen zu, bringt auf dasselbe
15 ctm hoch Mistbeeterde und scharrt dieselbe so zusammen, daß sich unter der
Mitte jedes Fensters ein Wall befindet, der von der Vorder- bis zur Hinterwand
reicht. Auf jeden dieser Wälle werden 2 Reihen Bohnen gesät. Das Luftgeben

S. 114

hängt von der Witterung ab, bei hellem Wetter wird gespritzt, nur nicht
während der Blüthe.
Nach je einigen Wochen werden noch mehrere Kästen mit Mist angelegt und
mit Bohnen bepflanzt, bis zum Auspflanzen der Bohnen ins Freie.

Für die Erbeertreiberei befindet sich in *Knowsley* gleichfalls kein besonderes
Haus, dieselben werden, wie die Bohnen, in anderen Häusern nebenbei
getrieben.
Zum Zweck der Treibens werden im August kräftige Ausläufer auf ein
wohlvorbereitetes Beet gepflanzt und bis zum Winter sorgfältig gepflegt.
Im Winter wird das Beet mit kurzem verrottetem Pferdemist bedeckt. Im
April des folgenden Jahres werden die besten Pflanzen davon in Töpfen, in
einer Mischung von Laub-

S. 115

und Mistbeeterde gepflanzt und im Küchengarten längs der Wege aufgestellt;
sorgfältig gegossen und schlechte Blätter, sowie sich bildende Ausläufer, abge-
kniffen. Im Juli werden sie verpflanzt und bleiben nun an ihrem Platze stehen,
bis sie zum Treiben in die resp. Häuser genommen werden.
Im Spätherbst, bei Eintritt kalter Witterung, werden sie mit Laub bedeckt.
Zum ersten Treiben wird *Black Prince* benutzt, diese Sorte trägt reichlich
kleine Früchte von leidlichem Wohlgeschmack.

Die Töpfe werden Mitte October in das Ananashaus gebracht, wo sie auf
2 über dem Mittelgang angebrachten Brettern Platz finden (Vgl. Fig. P).
Für das zweite Treiben benutzt man *Keen's Seedling,*

S. 116

eine der besten Treiberdbeeren; für die Töpfe befindet sich ein Brett an der
Hinterwand des zweiten Weintreibhauses (vrgl. Fig. G).
Im Feigenhause befinden sich über dem Gange Bretter zum dritten, im
Kirschhaus zum vierten Treiben; zu ersterem wird *Duc de Malakoff* benutzt,
zu letzterem nimmt man *Oscar* und *Heywood prolific;* alle 3 Sorten sind sehr
empfehlenswerth.
Nach diesen wird *President* mit großer, feiner Frucht im Weinhaus Nr. 6 des
Planes getrieben. Daran schließt sich *Sir Charles Napier* in den Weinhäu-
sern Nr. 1 und 2 des Planes, und zum letzten Treiben wird *Dr. Hogg,* eine
der schönsten und besten Erdbeeren verwendet; die Töpfe werden in
das Kirschhaus und in das Feigenhaus gestellt, nachdem *Duc de Malakoff,
Heywood prolific* und *Oscar* abgeerntet.

S. 117

Der <u>Gemüseanbau</u> ist in *Knwosley* im Allgemeinen derselbe wie hier.
Rhabarber wird in großen Massen, der Blattstiele wegen, angebaut, ebenso
Sellerie, wozu man die durch Zusammenbinden des Laubes gebleichten,
sehr wohlschmeckenden jungen Blattstiele ohne weitere Zubereitung mit
Salz genießt und zwar gewöhnlich mit Brunnenkresse und Senf zusammen,
welche letztere man alle 8–14 Tage in Kästchen sät, um den ganzen Winter
über junge Pflanzen zu haben.
Die <u>Champignon-Zucht</u> unterscheidet sich nicht von der hiesigen. In dem
Wirthschaftsgebäude i des Planes befindet sich ein abgeschlossener dunkler
Raum, in welchem 4 Champignonbeete von circa 10 m Länge sich befinden;
sie

S. 118

Sie [*sic*] werden vom Herbst bis zum Frühjahr abwechselnd mit frischem
Pferdemist gefüllt, welchen man fest walzt. Wenn der Mist sich auf etwa 22°R
abgekühlt hat, werden in die Oberfläche des Beetes die Brutsteinstücke flach
eingescharrt. Sobald der Mist mit Brutfäden durchzogen ist (nach etwa 10
Tagen) wird auf das Beet ein Gemisch von Laub und Rasenerde 5 ctm hoch
aufgeschüttet und leicht angedrückt. Bis zum Erscheinen der jungen Pilze
wird das Beet von Zeit zu Zeit mit lauwarmem Wasser überspritzt.

Bei meiner Rückkehr von England nach Deutschland hielt ich mich, wie bei der Hinreise, einige Tage in London auf, um daselbst die berühmten *Kew-gardens* mit den vorzüglichen, reichhaltigen Museen, dem schönen, großen Palmen-

S. 119

hause, der unübertrefflichen Farnsammlung etc. sowie die großen Etablissements von *Veitch, Bull, Williams* und *Henderson* wiederholt zu besuchen.

Leider war meine Zeit zu knapp zugemessen um mich in den genannten Etablissements und in dem botanischen Garten mit seinen reichen Pflanzenschätzen so gründlich umzusehen, wie ich es gern gethan hätte, doch hatte ich immerhin schon vielfach Gelegenheit, mir äußerst interessante Notizen über Pflanzenculturen, Verbreitung von Nutzgewächsen (im *Kew-Museum*) etc. zu machen, sowie, Culturpflanzen aller Arten in außerordentlicher Vollkommenheit zu sehen, ebenso viele <u>Neuheiten</u> in großen und schönen Exemplaren, von denen ich zum

S. 120

Schluß noch einige nennen will:

Allocasia Marshalli

  ″   *illustris,* beide sind *A. Jenningsii,* ähnlich gezeichnet, doch hat *A. Marshalli* bedeutend größere Blätter, während *illustris* sich durch einen silbergrauen Fleck in der Mitte des Blattes von *A. Jenningsii* unterscheidet.

Von *Anthurium Scherzerianum album* sah ich ein sehr starkes Exemplar bei *William,* welches jedoch leider nicht blüthe, als ich dort war.

Croton limbatum, die dunkelgrünen Blätter haben eine dunkelgelbe Mittelrippe, eben solche Flecke und röthlich-gelbe Ränder.

Croton majesticum hat schmale, sehr lange Blätter, die jüngeren sind gelb, die älteren roth gezeichnet.

Croton spirale, mit schraubenzieherförmigen Blättern.

S. 121

Croton volutum mit rückwärts gerollten, bunten Blättern, weniger schön als sonderbar.

Curculigo recurvata striala, vom Habitus der gewöhnlichen *C. r.,* die Blätter haben weiße Streifen in der Richtung der Adern.

Cyrtanthera chryostephana mit schönem, goldgelbem Blüthenstand.

Dioscorea illustrata hat große Blätter, welche oben schön grün und silbergrau gefleckt, unten roth sind.

Hibiscus puniceus mit leuchtend karminrothen großen Blüthen,
Hibiscus miniatus semiplenus, gleichfalls sehr schön,
Kentia Canterburyana, eine sehr elegante Palme.
Macrozamia cylindrica,
     "   *corallipes,*
     "   *plumosa.*
Letztere ist wohl eine der schönsten Cycadeen.

S. 122

Maranta Mackoyana findet man in England, wie in Belgien schon in sehr großen schönen Exemplaren, ebenso:
Maranta hieroglyphica
Maranta Semanni hat schöne sammetartige grüne Blätter mit heller Mittelrippe, Unterseite roth,
Musa Africana, mit rothen Blattstielen,
Pandanus Veitchii, den *P. Javanicus var.* an Schönheit weit übertreffend,
Poinsettia pulcherrima mit dem leuchtend rothen Blätterkranz, der den Blüthenstand umgiebt, läßt sich leicht durch Stecklinge vermehren,
Pteris serrulata cristata variegata,
Spathiphyllum pictum, mit sehr schön gezeichneten Blättern.

PLATE 5

Fig. A

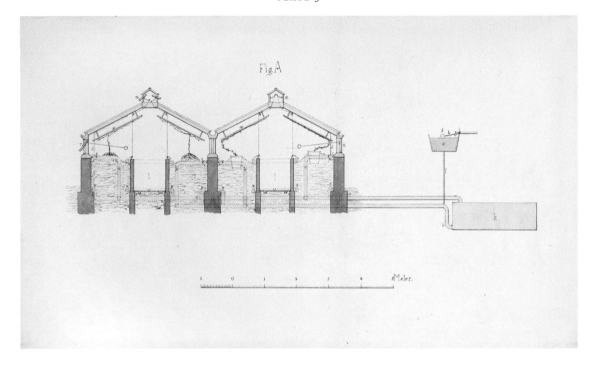

PLATE 6

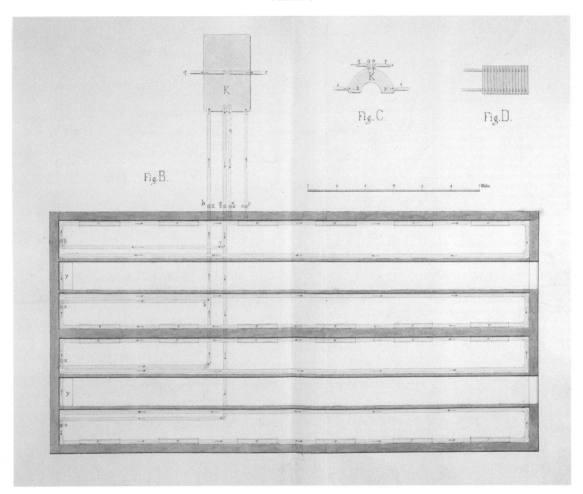

Fig.B.

Fig.C.

Fig.D.

PLATE 7

49

Fig. E.

⅕ des Holzes, der Länge
nach, glatt abgeschnitten
(siehe Fig. E). Man schneidet die Augen in der
ersten Hälfte des Ja-
nuar und legt sie so-
gleich in einem mit
Flußsand gefüllten,
und mit gutem Ab-
zug versehenen Ka-
sten so, wayrecht hin-
ein, daß wir das Auge
selbst die Oberfläche
des Sandes überragt,
und daß jedes Auge
vom andern einen
Abstand von 4-5 Centi-
metern hat. Der Ka-
sten wird an einem
warmen Platz (Gär-
tenhaus) gestellt. So-
bald die Augen 5-10
Centimeter lang aus-
getrieben, werden sie
in Töpfe von 4-5 cm.
Weite gepflanzt, in ei-
ne Mischung von san-
digem Lehm, Lau-
pferde und Borll-
schütt. Wenn sie gut
durchgewurzelt, pflanzt

PLATE 8

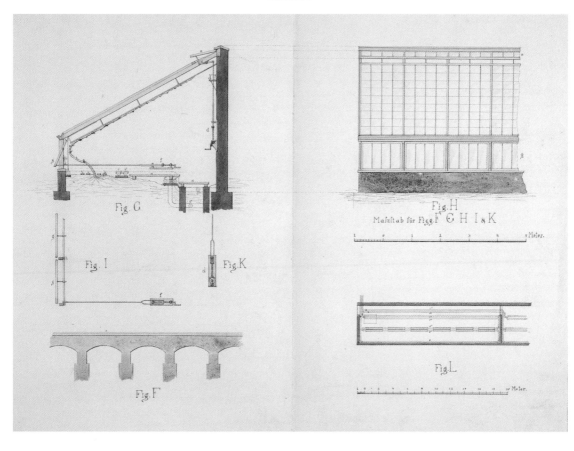

Fig. G

Fig. I

Fig. K

Fig. F

Fig. H

Maßstab für Figg. F G H I & K

Fig. L

PLATE 9

Fig. F. 1.

PLATE 10

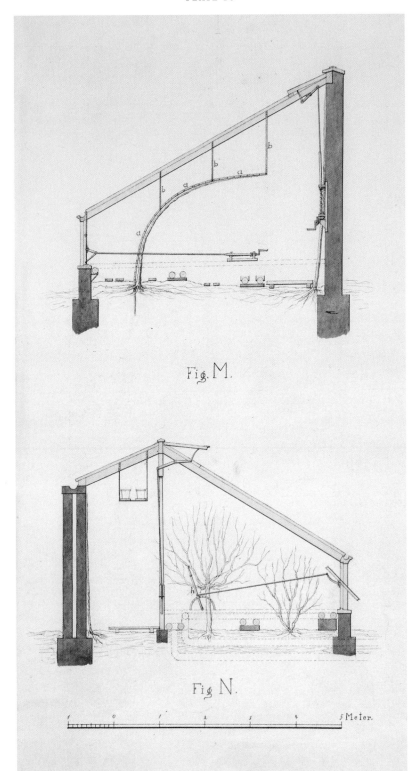

Fig. M.

Fig. N.

PLATE 11

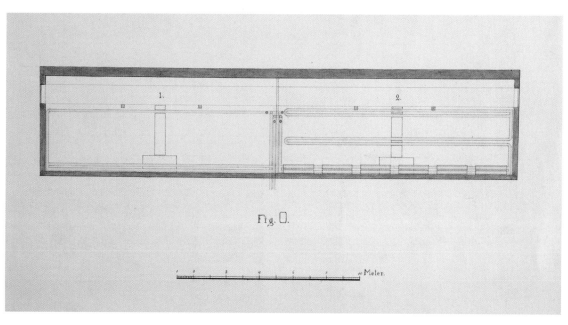

Fig. O.

PLATE 12

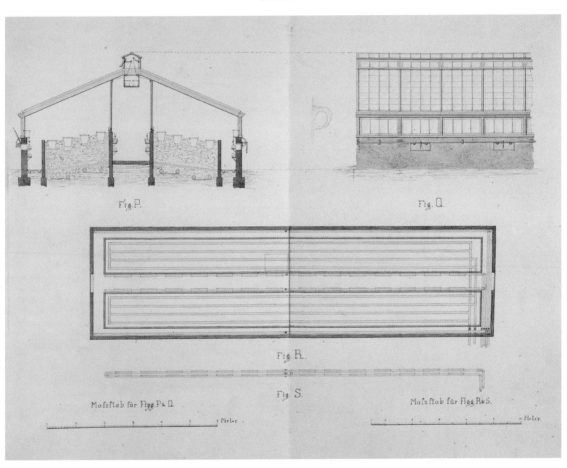

Fig. P.

Fig. Q.

Fig. R.

Fig. S.

Mafzftab für Figg. P & Q.

Mafzftab für Figg. R & S.

Meter.

Meter.

PLATE 13

SITUATIONS-PLAN
der
KNOWSLEY-GARDENS
dem Earl of Derby gehörig

aufgenommen und gezeichnet
1874-1875 durch
H. Janeke.

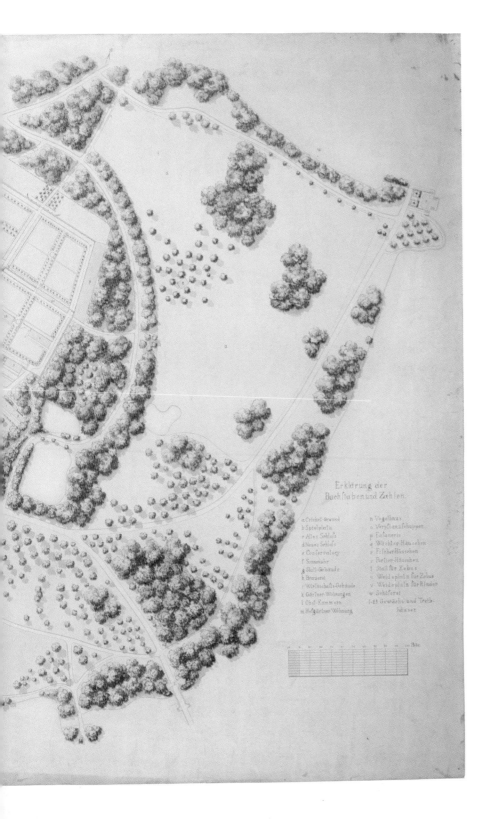

plate 13
Plan of the inner part of the
Knowsley Gardens, by Hans
Jancke, 1874. The inner part,
with kitchen, fruit, and flower
gardens, was separated from
the Knowsley Park. The
plan was later removed from
Jancke's travel report and
is currently in the archives
of the Stiftung Preußische
Schlösser und Gärten Berlin-
Brandenburg (SPSG), Nachlass
Jancke, GK II [1] 15103.
(Photograph: Daniel Lindner)

REPORT ON THE STUDY JOURNEY

HANS JANCKE,
author

JOACHIM WOLSCHKE-BULMAHN,
editor
MIC HALE,
translator

CONTENTS

[1] The lower right portion of the manuscript page is missing. The page numbers have been added in brackets.

P. 1

Sanssouci, June 1875

After I had returned from the field to complete my studies at the Königliche Gärtner-Lehranstalt that had been interrupted by the war with France, Herr Garten-Inspector *Gärdt* [2] graciously granted me a position in the nursery of Herr *Borsig* under his direction, where I worked for one year in the orchid- and hothouses. In the spring of 1873 I went thenceforth to Metz, there to work at the tree nursery of *Simon Louis Frères*, and found employment in the autumn of that same year at *Linden's* establishment near Ghent. Here I

P. 2

was delighted to receive, in February of 1874, news of a beneficent grant of 100 Thaler from the Königliche Gärtner-Lehranstalt for a study journey to England, conjoined with the injunction to compile a report of my experiences upon my return. Through the good offices of Königlicher Obergärtner Herr *Fintelmann* I was invited to take up employment at the *Knowsley Gardens* in the charge of *Mr. Harrison*, a property of the *Earl of Derby*, where I found ample opportunity to broaden my knowledge, whereof in the following, according to my commission, I humbly allow myself to give a closer account.

P. 3

The *Knowsley Gardens* lie in the finest part of the rainy county of *Lancashire*, in the midst of flourishing villages and extensive woodland. The terrain is of gently rolling hills, gradually undulating downward from north-northeast to south-southwest. Beautiful ancient trees, mostly *Acer, Aesculus, Castanea, Fagus, Quercus, Tilia & Ulmus* tower above the dense underbrush, which to the greatest extent consists of evergreen shrubs: *Ilex, Buxus, Cupressus, Thuja, Taxus,* and masses of *Rhododendron,* surrounding the kitchen-, fruit-, and flower garden, the fruit forcing houses, stalls, etc., while more recent plantings

2 Hans Jancke primarily used Old German letters in the travel report; he used modern writing only for personal, place, and plant names. These terms are marked in italics in the transcription.

of trees and shrubs, some evergreen, some deciduous, pleasantly punctuate the well-tended,

P. 4

perpetually lush green lawns surrounding the castle. The maritime climate with its mild winters makes it possible for a few specimens of *Araucaria imbricata* and *Cedrus Deodara* to thrive, while the cool summers do not promote the growth of trees with pinnate leaves and they are sparsely represented; *Robinia, Gleditschia,* and the like are completely absent. A few other trees, very common in our land, such as *Betula, Fraxinus,* and *Platanus* make a very weak showing here.
Soon after my arrival at Knowsley the wish grew in me to possess a plan of the inner park, and when one of my colleagues offered to assist me with the surveying

P. 5

and after acquiring a surveyor's chain and cross-staff—the purchase of a compass or a theodolite, which would have eased the survey greatly, was beyond my means—we set to work and had, during our free time almost every day after work, completed almost half the task we had set ourselves. Then my assistant was hindered from carrying on with our surveying so that I was thrown back upon my own resources. At first I considered it almost impossible to complete the work without help, especially as I also had to use my free time on the one hand to write up my notes on the plant forcing, on the other hand to revise what I had learned earlier, but

P. 6

eventually I brought the work to its desired conclusion and was in a position to complete the plan from my draft; I enclose it with my report. For a closer understanding of the same I permit myself the following explanatory remarks: The *Knowsley Gardens* are completely separated from the adjacent *Knowsley Park* by iron railings, their main purpose being to prevent the incursions of the numerous red and fallow deer. The *Gardens* are bordered on two sides by lakes (A, B, C & D on the plan), notable less for their fine forms as for their extraordinarily clear, clean water and enormous stocks of fish. The houses and lakes adjoining the *Gardens*

P. 7

are enclosed with masonry walls, bearing a part of the railings.
Lake A, bordering the garden to the east, is around six hundred meters long and 250 meters wide. On the opposite shore a range of low hills rise, which in summer is covered with head-high bracken (*Pteris aquilina*) that fructifies

abundantly every year; from this ground there rise numerous ancient coniferous and deciduous trees, overlooked by an old ruined tower. The lake offers a wonderful view from the fisherman's cottage r, in which splendid boats for pleasure trips in summer are kept. Lake A lies higher than the greater part of the garden

P. 8

and supplies the same by means of a many-branched system of pipes with clear, potable water. The paths that run along its shore are but a few meters above its surface. The water level of Lake B lies about sixteen meters lower than that of A, that of C yet another 1.5 meters lower than B, and the water level of D lies some four meters lower than that of C; unfortunately I lacked the time for a more precise measurement of the height differences, which I would dearly like to have made. The aforementioned lakes are connected with each other and with the four smaller ponds in the middle of the garden by robust underground pipes with stopcocks, by means of which sudden rises in the water levels in spring and already at the end of winter

P. 9

are controlled. Lake D has an outflow at its western end to the lakes in the outer park. As yet there are no fountains, although they could have been built quite easily and at no great expense but, as *Mr. Harrison* intimated to me, it is intended to erect a fountain in the next few years in place of the large Rhododendron bush, located at the center of the extensive flower parterre to the east of the castle. With regard to the plantings in the parterre, of the eight s-shaped beds four are usually planted with a centerline of *Achyranthes Verschaffetli* and a surround of *Pyrethrum*

P. 10

Parthenium var. aureum, the other four with *Iresine Lindeni* and *Gnaphalium tomentosum* as surround. The remaining beds are planted with Siarlat Pelargoniums;[3] in the summer of 1874 the following varieties were used:
Bonfire with large bright vermillion blooms was most frequently used after the bright red lead-colored *Warrior*, along with:
Excellent flesh-colored,
Janthe carmoisine red,
Blue Bell light carmoisine red,
Thomas Speed vermillion,
Jean Sisley red lead with a large white eye at its center,
Stella with small leaves but luminous dark red blooms,
Annie Hogg light red,
Mr Constance pale purple-colored,

3 Although Jancke clearly wrote Siarlat in the travel report, it is unclear if today Scarlet-Pelargoniums would be meant.

P. 11

Violet Hill flesh-colored.

Further varieties with multicolored blooms were also used:

Mrs. Pollock

Lady Cullum

Beauty of Caulderdale

Gem

Prince's Silver-Wing.

With gold-edged leaves:

Crystal Palace Gem,

Golden Chain,

with silver-edged leaves:

Silver Queen

Flower of Spring

Flower of the Day

Waltham Bride

The beds planted with Pelargoniums are partly enclosed with *Lobelia Erinus,* partly with *Gnaphalium lanatum* or *Echeveria metallica glauca.* The following plants were used in the round and elliptical beds on either side of the path directly

P. 12

adjacent to the south side of the parterre:

Ageratum Mexicanum Imperial Dwarf.

Calceolaria floribunda

Centaurea gymnocarpa

Lobelia Erinus

Perilla Nankinensis

Tagetes patula

Heliotropium Peruvianum

along with the aforementioned Pelargoniums and diverse Petunia varieties.

The two round groups further to the back were planted with numerous varieties of *Canna Indica* and *Gladiolus.*

To the north of the parterre described above lies the <u>*Conservatory*</u>, consisting of a hot and a camellia section and connected to the castle by a corridor. In each section there is a central bed and two side

P. 13

beds in which some very fine and valuable plants stand. Among the plants to be found in the hothouse section one may mention as worthy of recommendation: four very vigorous specimens of *Musa Cavendishi*, which bear fruit annually, two large specimens of *Cycas revoluta*, and additionally

Hedychium Gardnerianum
Alpinia nutans
Bambusa gracilis
Coffea Arabica also bearing fruit every year,
Strelitzia ovata
Citrus Limonum
Plumbago Capensis
Clerodendron Balfouri
Bougainvillea glabra
Dipladenia amabilis
Thunbergia Harrissii
Passiflora quadrangularis & edulis, of the latter I pollinated some flowers
with pollen from *quadrangularis*, all of which

P. 14

developed fruit, which unfortunately had not quite ripened before my
departure. Mention should also be made of:
Bactris Maraja
Kentia Balmoreana
Daemonorops melanochaetes
Euterpe edulis
Livistona Australis
Areca Verschaffelti
Ceroxylon niveum
Chamaedorea graminifolia
Sabal umbraculifera
Welfia regia
Zalacca Wagneri
Sphaerogyne latifolia
Cyanophyllum magnificum
Pandanus Javanicus varieg.
      "   *graminifolius*
Hibiscus puniceus
Dichorisandra thyrsiflora
Euphorbia Jacquiniaeflora
Rivinia humilis
Rogiera cordata
Asclepias Curassavica
Stephanotis floribunda
The back wall is wreathed in *Habrothamnus elegans* and *Clerodendron
Balfouri*.

P. 15

In the side beds one finds:
Gymnogramme sulphurea
    "   *ochracea*
    "   *Laucheana*
Neottopteris nidus-avis
Doryopteris palmata
Asplenium Bellangeri
Cyrtomium falcatum
Pteris longifolia and others.
The soil of all three beds is thickly covered with *Selaginella denticulata, Oplismenes variegata, Tradescantia zebrina, Fittonia argyroneura & rubrovenosa.* Above the paths on both sides of the central bed hang finely woven wire baskets containing *Hoya bella, Ardisia crenata, Russellia juncea,* etc. The central bed of the cooler section is planted with Camellias, while the back wall is clad with:

P. 16

Luculia gratissima
Acacia armata
    "   *oleifolia*
    "   *pubescens*
Habrothamnus elegans
Kennedya Maryatta and another variety of *Kennedya* grown from seed at *Knowsley* of vigorous growth and cloudy red blooms.
As a creeper, the lovely but unfortunately still rare here *Tacsonia van Volxemii* is used extensively. In the side beds grow: *Aspidium, Pteris, Scolopendrium,* etc., a few specimens of *Thea Bohea* and *Thea viridis* standing in between them and also, according to the time of year, diverse pot plants are set out: *Heliotropium, Fuchsia, Pelargonium, Chrysanthemum, Cytisus,* etc.
The corridor is graced with Camellias in pots, along with:

P. 17

Fuchisa and *Pelargonium, Lobelia fulgens, Acacia armata, Lapageria rosea & alba, Clianthus magnificus, Agave Americana* and *A. A. variegata*; the two last mentioned are never set out of doors.
To the north of the castle lies the <u>Kitchen Garden</u> with well-tended fruit plantings, greenhouses and forcing houses, hotbeds, etc. The south-facing walls of the Kitchen Garden are clad half with <u>peaches</u> and half with apricot and pear trees.

The former are entirely trained in fans, with the following varieties:

Noblesse, early fruiting and very suitable for forcing,

Royal George, also much used for forcing,

Bellegarde, equally worthy of recommendation, well suited for transporting as it keeps longer after picking than the other varieties,

Violette hâtive ripens in September,

Early Beatrice, early and very sweet,

Salway, Dagmar & Walburton, of the latter three there were only young specimens that had not yet borne fruit. <u>Nectarines</u> present were:

Elruge, very fine and highly suitable for early forcing,

Large Elruge

Stanwick Elruge

Pitmaston Orange early and prolific, ripens in August and September,

Albert Victor, fine and very large, ripens in early September.

Of the <u>Apricots</u> only three varieties were grown, namely:

Moorpark, bears large quantities

of fine fruit and is by all means worthy of recommendation,

Turkey, equally recommendable, with a slightly sour taste.

Persian Apricot

The <u>Pears</u> cultivated against the south walls are, in the order in which they ripen, as follows:

Williams's bon chrétien, provides great quantities of delicious fruit in August already,

British Queen, September,

Duchesse d'Angoulême, bore only a few fruit in the previous year at *Knowsley* and would only, I was told, provide a good yield in exceptionally warm years,

Gansels Bergamot, bore no good fruit,

Marie Louise is only bettered in its copious yield by *Glout Morceau,* while they

are probably equal in the goodness of their fruit,

B. Diel bears large fruit at *Knowsley* too.

Passe Colmar bears a good yield against the walls.

Glout Morceau is one of the most highly prized winter pears in *Lancashire,* bearing an exceptionally rich yield of large, fine fruit that keeps very well.

Winter Nélis, also an excellent winter pear,

Ne plus meuris ripens in March,
Beurré de Rance keeps until May.
The east-facing walls are used exclusively for pears; here are to be found the following varieties, again in the order in which they ripen:
Williams's bon chrétien
Jargonelle, good,
Summer Frank Real bears

P. 21

small but very juicy and sweet fruit,
Beurré d'Amanlis, probably one of the best summer pears,
Beurré superfin, large and good,
Beurré de Capiaumont, high yield,
Aston Town with small but fine fruit, also in large quantities,
Duchesse d'Angoulême
Thompsons, good,
Gansels Bergamot,
Crassanne bears plentiful fruit against the walls,
Forelle, plentiful, beautifully colored,
Winter Nélis,
Josephine de Malines, good,
Easter Beurré good against the walls,
Baronne de Mello, large and good,
Additionally, there are a few young trees by the old walls that have not yet borne fruit:
Black Styrian,
Moccas,

P. 22

Knight's Monarch.
Although the pears grown against the eastern walls were not entirely comparable in taste and size with those on the southerly walls, they still markedly exceeded that of those grown in pyramid form; this was apparent with *Passe Colmar, Cassanne,* and *Glout Morceau.*
Against the walls a few single trees were trained in fan shape and in oblique palmette form; all the rest were trained in horizontal palmettes.
The pear trees in pyramid form are located in the narrow beds on either side of the Kitchen Garden paths, alternating with apple trees. The following varieties are cultivated in pyramid form at *Knowsley*:
Doyonné d'Été, the most prolific of the summer pears,

Jargonelle, highly recommended, began to sprout as early as the end of January
this year,
Williams's bon chrétien
Brockworth Park
British Queen
Beurré d'Amanlis
Doyenné blanc, attractive, heavy yield,
Fondante d'Automne, one of the best pears for October,
Jersey Gratioli
Baronne de Mello
Swan's Egg
Louise bonne de Jersey, very fine and very prolific,
Duchesse d'Angoulême
Marie Louise, even though it does not grow attractively as a pyramid it
produces good yields,
Comte de Lamy, very good
Délices d'Hardenpont, good, fine-looking and prolific,
Passe Colmar, less good as a pyramid than against a wall,
Crassanne,

Colmar d'Aremberg, very coarse flesh,
Glout Monceau, although not quite as good as against the wall, it can still hold its
own on taste with all other varieties and surpass most of them as regards yield,
Doyenné du Comice bore only a few, but very good, fruits.
Huyshe's Victoria
Alexandre Lambre
Winter Nélis
Zephirin Grégoire has a very fine aroma, small fruit,
General Todtleben
Bellissime d'hiver
Many recently planted pyramids of *Délices de Jodoigne* and *Huyshe's Bergamot*
were not yet bearing fruit.
Along with these varieties trained against walls and in pyramids, pears were
also trained on freestanding espaliers, on either side

of the main path through the Kitchen Garden in the following varieties:
Beurré superfin

Beurré Hardy

Swan's Egg

Louise bonne de Jersey bore very large quantities of fine fruit

Flemish Beauty, also good,

Jersey Gratioli

Duchesse d'Angoulême

Marie Louise, also here splendid and prolific,

Jalousie de Fontenay

Passe Colmar bore poorly,

Triomphe de Jodoigne

Délices d'Hardenpont, good,

Colmar d'Aremberg

Napoléon, good,

Prince of Wales

Glout Morceau, excellent, as it is against the walls

Hacons Incomparable

Colmar, not as good here as against the walls,

Winter Beurré bore plentiful small fruit with a fine aroma,

Winter Nélis, very fine,

P. 26

Josephine de Malines bore a rich harvest of splendid fruit.
A young *Suffolk Thorn* tree was planted that had not yet borne fruit but was recommended as good. Although the yield from the *Knowsley* pear trees cannot compare with that achieved in Belgium, and particularly France and Lorraine, the reason is probably to be found solely in the moist climate and the less warm summers, and the harvest is still such that one could regard the means employed and the trouble taken as receiving its reward. The yield of some varieties grown against the walls could be described as very heavy, while less good on the freestanding espaliers while still more prolific than those on the

P. 27

trees trained in pyramid form.
The ground at *Knowsley* is generally a heavy, humus-rich clay soil, which has been made more suitable for fruit cultivation by excellent drainage. The pears are, as already mentioned, mostly trained in horizontal palmette and pyramid shapes, and pruning is on the whole the same as here. One begins the spring pruning at the end of January. The central leaders are left on average longer than with us to encourage good fruitwood, as the moist climate and heavy soil promotes less the fruit set than the sprouting wood;

for the same reason horizontal palmettes are preferred above all other forms on the walls and espaliers;

P. 28

the horizontal arrangement of the branches is most favorable to the fruit set.

In May the tips of the younger shoots are pinched out.

In August the summer shoots are cut back to around half their length; thus the buds on the lower half develop into leaf and blossom buds.

In October the fruiting shoots are pruned back to four or five bud collars, and those which are too strong are even cut back to the branch collar.

As already mentioned above, along with the pear tree pyramids there are also apple trees, some of them standard trees, some in low pyramid form, some also in cylindrical form, in the beds on either side of the Kitchen Garden paths, furthermore some beds

P. 29

are enclosed by <u>apple trees</u> trained in horizontal step-over form; the pruning of which, as with the pears, does not differ from the principles applied here. The apple yield is relatively higher than that of the pears. The varieties cultivated at *Knowsley* are, in the order in which they ripen, as follows:

Early Harvest, very good, already ripening by the end of July,

Lord Suffield, good commercial apple,

Duchess of Oldenburgh, medium-sized, fine taste,

Summer Golden Pipin [*sic*], very good, trained in garland form,

White Astrachan, very good,

Scarlet Parmain

Cellini

Gravenstein, very good,

Hawthornden, large commercial apple,

P. 30

King of Pippins, good, heavy yield,

Flower of Kent, large commercial apple, heavy yield,

Franklin's golden Pippin

Essex Pippin, small,

Beauty of Kent, large and of fine appearance, but not very tasty,

Ribston Pippin, very heavy yield,

Northern Spy, very good,

Lord Derby, large commercial apple,

Cox's Orange Pippin, fine appearance and taste,

Blenheim orange Pippin, large and good as a pyramid and garland,
Court pendu plat, good, heavy yield,
Lewis's incomparable, large,
Rosemary Russet, very fine,
Golden Russet, very palatable,
Dutch Mignonne, with a fine aroma, heavy yield,
Cornish Gilliflower trained as a step-over low tree,
Scarlet Nonpareil
White Calville, bears no

P. 31

good fruit at *Knowsley,*
Old Nonpareil, heavy yield,
Boston Russet, very good.
The western walls of the Kitchen Garden are planted with plum and cherry trees of the following varieties:
1. Plums:
Green Gage (early *Reine Claude*) ripens in mid-August against the walls.
Coe's late red with small, red, not very attractive fruit, does not ripen until November,
Jefferson bore plentiful large, yellow, red-spotted, very sweet fruit and ripens, as do all the following, in September,
Denyers Victoria
Coe's golden drop bore very fine and palatable fruit in large quantities,
Transparent Gage, with large fine-looking fruit with a good taste,
Kukes plum, large, blue and

P. 32

very juicy fruits, very prolific,
2. Cherries
Belle d'Orleans, very fine in appearance and early, ripening in mid-June,
Black Tartarian, very prolific, end of June,
May Duke much used for forcing.
The northern side of the walls and the back walls of the houses are not left unused; against them are planted Morello cherries and blackcurrants. The former are all trained in extremely well-developed fan shapes. In the autumn after the summer shooting any overly dense growth of shoots is removed; there is no spring pruning.
The blackcurrants are trained in a simple U form and are used like the Amarelle[4] cherries in jam making.
Proceeding now to the

4 Jancke in this instance describes the cherries on the north-facing walls as Amarelle, the light-fleshed variety of sour cherry; however, in the previous lines he refers to them as Morello.

plant and forcing houses:

Houses 1–10 on the plan are <u>grapevine glasshouses</u>

Nos. 11 and 12 are <u>peach houses</u>,

No. 13 is a <u>melon house</u>,

No. 14 is a <u>propagation house</u>

Nos. 15–19 are <u>plant houses</u>.

In No. 20 (*Orchard house*) are peaches, plums, and cherries.

No. 21 is the <u>pineapple house</u>

No. 22 is the <u>cucumber house</u>

No. 23 is a <u>grapevine house</u>

No. 24 is the <u>cherry house</u>

No. 25 is the <u>fig house</u>.

All the houses, along with the <u>stone frames</u> in front of No. 14 and in front of and behind No. 21, are heated by a <u>hot-water system</u>: a <u>single</u> boiler, in fact, always supplies two or more houses (which can lie twenty to thirty meters apart) through pipes that run below ground. In this manner the grapevine houses Nos. 1 and 2

share a furnace, as do Nos. 3 and 4. Houses 5 and 6 are heated from the furnace behind No. 5 house, while a larger boiler (behind No. 9) supplies heat to grapevine houses Nos. 7, 8 & 9, the cherry house (No. 24), and the fig house (No. 25). The heating for the peach house (No. 12) and the cucumber house (13), the pineapple house and the frames in front of and behind it is behind No. 12 house. Behind No. 10 is the boiler from which grapevine houses Nos. 11 and 12, the cool house, No. 14,[5] and the frames in front of it are heated, while the heating for the propagation house, No. 15, cool houses Nos. 16 and 17, the cucumber house (No. 22), and the grapevine house (No. 23) is between houses 16 and 17. For the orchid house (18) and hothouse (19)

and the frames in front of them the heating plant is behind No. 18.

Of the two <u>plant houses</u> Nos. 18 and 19 the former is warmer and contains namely plants from East India and the South Sea Islands, notably:

Aerides Fieldingii

    "   *odoratum*

    "   *quinquevulnerum*

    "   *Schroederi*

    "   *suavissimum*

    "   *virens*

Angrecum eburneum

5 Above it states that No. 14 is the propagation house and that No. 15 is simply a plant house.

Porassia brachyata
Goodyera Dawsoniana
Phalaenopsis amabilis
       "   *grandiflora aurea*
       "   *Schilleriana*
Renanthera coccinea
Saccolabium Blumei
       "   *giganteum*
Vanda Batemanni
       "   *gigantea*
       "   *Lowii*
       "   *Roxburghii*

P. 36

Vanda suavis
   "   *teres*
   "   *tricolor*
Nepenthes ampullacea
       "   *Phyllamphora*
       "   *Rafflesiana*
Croton irregulare
       "   *interruptum*
       "   *majesticum*
       "   *maximum*
       "   *spirale*
       "   *undulatum*
       "   *Veitchii*
       "   *Weissmanni*
Ataccia cristata
Dracaena amabilis
       "   *Cooperi*
       "   *Guilfolei*
       "   *reginae*
       "   *Youngei*
Clerodendron Balfourei
       "   *fallax*
Anthurium leuconeurum
       "   *magnificum*
       "   *pedato-radiatum*
       "   *regale*
       "   *Scherzerianum*

Allocasia metallica
Sonerilla margaritacea
etc. etc. etc.
In No. 19

P. 37

are to be found the following notable plants:
Ada aurantiaca
Calanthe Masuca
    "   *Veitchii*
    "   *veratrifolia*
    "   *vestita*
Cattleya Aclandiae
    "   *bicolor*
    "   *Forbesii*
    "   *Gigas*
    "   *labiata*
    "   *maxima*
    "   *Mossiae*
    "   "   *superba*
    "   *quadricolor*
    "   *Skinneri*
    "   *Trianaei*
    "   *Wagneri*
Coelogyne cristata
Cymbidium giganteum
Cypripedium barbatum
    "   *barbatum majus*
    "   *concolor*
    "   *hirsutum*
    "   *Hookerii*
    "   *insigne*
    "   *Javanicum*
    "   *niveum*
    "   *Pearcei*
    "   *Roezlei*

P. 38

Cypripedium Stonei
    "   *venustum*
    "   *villosum*

Selenipedium caudatum
   "   *Schlimii*
Dendrobium chrysanthum
   "   *Dalhousianum*
   "   *densiflorum*
   "   *Devonianum*
   "   *Farmerii*
   "   *fimbriatum oculatum*
   "   *infundibilum*
   "   *macranthum*
   "   *nobile*
   "   *Paxtoni*
Epidendrum aurantiacum
   "   *ciliare*
   "   *fragrans*
   "   *prismatocarpum*
Houlletia Brocklehourstiana
Laelia acuminata
  "   *anceps*
  "   *autumnalis*
  "   *crispa*
  "   *majalis*
  "   *purpurea*
Leptotes bicolor
Lycaste Skinneri
Masdevallia ignea
Maxillaria picta
  "   *venusta*

P. 39

Mesopinidium sanguineum
   "   *vulcanium*
Miltonia candida
  "   *Moreliana purpurea*
  "   *spectabilis*
Odontoglossum Alexandrae
   "   *Bictoniense*
   "   *citrosmum*
   "   *Ehrenbergii*
   "   *gloriosum*
   "   *grande*

    "   *Insleayi*

    "   *Pescatorei*

    "   *Phalaenopsis*

    "   *pulchellum*

    "   *triumphans*

    "   *vexillarium*

Oncidium ampliatum

    "   *bifolium*

    "   *cucullatum*

    "   *Lanceanum*

    "   *ornithorrhynchum*

    "   *sphacelatum*

    "   *uniflorum*

Phajus grandifolius

    "   *maculatus*

    "   *Wallichii*

Pilumna fragrans

Pleione humilis

    "   *maculata*

Polycycnis barbata

P. 40

Sobralia macrantha

    "   *violacea*

Sophronites grandiflora

Trichopilia coccinea

    "   *suavis*

    "   *tortilis*

Zygopetalum Mackayi

    "   *maxillare*

along with the aforementioned *Croton* and *Dracaena*

Maranta Legrelleana

    "   *illustris*

    "   *Chimboracensis*

    "   *Mackoyana*

    "   *hieroglyphica*

    "   *tubispatha*

    "   *Veitchii*

    "   *princeps*

    "   *regalis*

    "   *vittata*

" 　setosa
　" 　cinerea
　" 　discolor
　" 　amabilis
　" 　argyrea
　" 　eximia
　" 　micans
　" 　Lindeni
　" 　fasciata
　" 　roseopicta
　" 　Wallisii

P. 41

Maranta virginalis major
　" 　zebrina
　" 　van den Heckii
　" 　splendida
　" 　smaragdina
Aphelandra aurantiaca
Aralia leptophylla
　" 　reticulata
Bilbergia zebrina
Nidularium fulgens
Tillandria Lindeni
　" 　musaica
　" 　tesselata
Vriesia psittacina
Calamus ciliaris
Cocos Weddeliana
Pandanus Veitchii
Coccoloba plalyclada
Cyrtanthera chrysostephana
Dalechampia Roezleana
Dipladenia amabilis
Epiphyllum truncatum trained along a wire, eight meters long.
Eranthemum pulchellum
Eucharis Amazonica
Franciscea confertiflora
Garcinia Livingstonei

Gardenia citriodora
       "   *Fortunei*
       "   *radicans*
Hibiscus puniceus

P. 42

Ixora coccinea
Pancratium fragrans
Pentas Kermesina
Phyllotaenium Lindenii
Tabernomontana coronaria
Thyrsacanthus rutilans
Additionally, No. 19 houses a fine collection of Caladiums on show:
Caladium argyrites
       "   *Auber*
       "   *Beethoven*
       "   *Belleymii*
       "   *Brogniardtii*
       "   *Chantini*
       "   *Meyerbeer*
       "   *Prince Albert Edward*
       "   *Wrightii, etc.*
The walled frames and cold houses provide temporary accommodation for *Erica, Poinsettia, Pelargonium, Cineraria, Calceolaria, Bouvardia,* etc. In the forcing houses, the following fruits are forced:
grapes, peaches, pineapples, cherries, figs, cucumbers. Their houses are also used to force strawberries and beans.

P. 43

Many of the houses, namely the newer ones, are constructed in exemplary fashion, and I have therefore executed precise drawings of some of them, which I include in the single chapters on the forcing of diverse species of fruit. Pride of place in fruit forcing at *Knowsley* is assumed by grapevine forcing. As the climate of northern England precludes the cultivation of grapevines outdoors, vine forcing is pursued with enormous diligence and with such success that the grapes grown there not only equal but even surpass in size, coloration, and taste those of lands whose climate is far more propitious for viniculture.

P. 44

In the royal gardens as well as in those of wealthy private persons and numerous commercial gardens in England the first ripe grapes are brought on in March by means of early forcing and, as the varieties which ripen last may be conserved with a little care until this time, one then has a supply of ripe grapes the whole year round.

Fig. A1 shows a section of the house used at *Knowsley Gardens* for the first grapevine forcing (Plan No. 23; Fig. A2 = Plan No. 22 is the cucumber house). Heating the houses happens here, as is almost always the case in England, by means of hot-water pipes. At A in Figure A hot water enters from the upper part of the boiler K,

P. 45

gives the greater part of its heat up to the iron pipes and the house, becomes heavier as it cools and flows through the gradually downward-sloping pipes to b and back into the lower part of the boiler, is reheated, rises once again, and continues around the cycle.

On the iron pipes there are containers c,c,c, which are filled with water which, as it evaporates, maintains a constant moistness in the air of the house. (Compare Figure B, which depicts the plan of the house with its heating pipes and boiler seen from above.)

The pipes d in Fig. A serve to permit air to leave the heating pipes when they are filled with water.

P. 46

The water in reservoir e through the pipes f ensures that the heating pipes are constantly full of water. The hollow copper sphere g floating on the water in the reservoir is connected by the arm k with the easily turned tap i; should the water level in e sink the sphere sinks with it and thereby opens the tap. By means of this apparatus, then, a certain water level is maintained in the reservoir, which one can alter at will by bending the arm h. One also finds this practical apparatus in all the basins inside the houses; by means of the continuous slow inflow the water is kept at as constant a temperature as possible, close to that of the house.

z in Fig. B are taps, by means of whose complete or

P. 47

partial opening or closing the temperature of the houses can be easily regulated with the greatest precision. y in Figure B are water reservoirs. Ventilation is effected by means of the apparatus m and n in Figure A, l is the path between the beds u, containing the grapevines. The beds are filled with dead leaves and horse manure, into which one sets the pot-grown vines. On the floor of the beds are iron pipes to provide constant heat (o & p in Figs. A & B) which are also heated by hot water from the boiler K.

Fig. C is a vertical section through the boiler K, the pipes

P. 48

a, b, o & p correspond to those identically labeled in Figs. A and B.

Houses 15, 16, and 17 are heated by the pipes q, r, s, and t.

Fig. D is the plan of a piece of walkway marked v in Fig. A; similar walkways are much used in English houses. For early forcing, young vine stocks in pots are used, and are discarded once they have borne fruit. Their propagation is from buds.

The buds from sturdy vines that have been pruned in late autumn or winter are cut out in such a fashion that around 1.5 centimeters of wood remains on either side. On the opposite side from the bud

P. 49

One-third of the wood is pared flat lengthwise (see Fig. E). One cuts the buds in the first half of January and lays them straightaway in a box filled with river sand and with good drainage so that only the bud itself protrudes above the surface of the sand and that each bud is spaced four to five centimeters from the next. The box is stood in a warm place in the cucumber house. As soon as the buds have sprouted some six to ten centimeters they are planted out in pots four to five centimeters apart in a mixture of sandy clay, compost, and limestone chippings. When they are well rooted they are planted

P. 50

in ten- and later in twenty-centimeter-diameter pots, in which they remain until the following year. With the advent of warmer weather they are set out in the open against a south-facing wall. When the wood is well matured one cuts the vines back to one or two buds and stores them in a frost-free place for the winter. In the following spring, when the buds have sprouted four to five centimeters and the roots are fully grown, the vines are repotted in thirty-centimeter-diameter pots in a mixture of sandy clay, compost, limestone chippings, and bone meal. Only the most vigorous shoot is left on the stock; the others are clipped and later cut off. As soon as the pots are well filled by the roots, they receive once or twice a week a

P. 51

watering with liquid fertilizer and are set out for the summer in a sheltered, sunny place.

Once the woody stock is matured the vines are cut back to between one and two meters and planted out at the end of October in beds prepared with manure and dead leaves (Fig. A).

In order to achieve even sprouting from all spurs and namely to restrain the uppermost spur to the advantage of the middle and lower spurs the vines are tied back (Fig. F1).

As soon as the pots are brought into the house, watering with dissolved manure is temporarily suspended. The temperature in the first week is 12°R[6] by day and 8° at night. The air in the house is kept constantly moist by sprinkling the soil and walls, and

P. 52

by filling the evaporating pans, while the vines themselves are sprayed mornings and afternoons with warm water (18–20°). The temperature is thereafter gradually raised to 16° during the day and 12° at night; when the sun shines this can rise by a constant 4–5°. As soon as the buds open and have sprouted by one to two centimeters the vines are carefully tied to the espaliers (w in Fig. A). When the bunches have markedly developed they are no longer sprayed and only the walls and floor are moistened. One leaves only three to four well-developed bunches, the tendril is pinched out two buds above the last bunch on the vine. During blossom time the temperature is maintained at 18°R during the day

P. 53

and 14° at night, and a little more ventilation is permitted to promote pollination, whereby one should not allow the air in the house to become too dry. Shortly after the flowers wilt one commences pruning the bunches: with scissors, one cuts out on average a third part of the bunch to allow the remainder more space and more nutrients. Raffia binding is used to carefully tie the upper twigs of the vine up and apart so that the separate grapes can develop fully without touching each other. After the wilt, one again waters the pots once a week with liquid fertilizer prepared from deer manure. As soon as the grapes begin to color,

P. 54

which occurs at the end of March, watering with dissolved manure is ceased and the temperatures reduced to 16° during the day and 12° at night, the same being maintained through to ripening. Throughout this entire period, from the beginning of coloring to ripeness, one keeps the house fairly dry and ensures plentiful ventilation; at night, too, this is not entirely suspended. In this manner one achieves a good color and fine aroma. When the grapes have

6 Jancke used the Réaumur temperature scale. 12°Réaumur equals 15° Celsius.

attained their full ripeness, by means of plentiful ventilation one keeps the house cool and dry in order to prolong the grape harvest as long as possible. Once the grapes have been picked the vines are thrown away.

The best varieties of vine, and those used most widely in England for early forcing,

P. 55

are: *Black Hamburgh* and *Foster's Seedling*; the former takes pride of place among the blue varieties, the latter among the whites.

Black Hamburg bears medium-sized bunches of medium-sized grapes and is worthy of high recommendation.

Foster's Seedling bears medium-sized bunches of three to four pounds in weight; the grapes are also of medium size, a delicate yellow, and very palatable. In the houses that are used for second and third forcings the vines "stand im Bande."[7] For propagation, at the end of February or beginning of March good buds from sturdy vines are planted in the aforementioned manner and treated identically over the following summer and winter. In the following spring the stocks are planted in the house designated for them,

P. 56

after the heavy clay soil has been dug out to a depth of one meter and mixed with plenty of limestone chippings and bone meal. Beneath each rafter and at the middle of each window one stock is planted, so that the distance between each plant is around 0.75 meter.

If the north wall of the house is built with openings [in the foundations] (see Fig. F) so that the roots can spread outside, something highly recommended in houses for later forcing, then one plants the stocks 0.3–0.5 meter from the same, while in houses with a solid front wall (e.g., Fig. G) one plants them 1–1.5 meters back from the wall so that the roots can spread in all directions. As soon as the buds have sprouted, one leaves just one spur

P. 57

on each stock. Throughout the summer the stocks are plentifully sprayed and aired, and the lead spur cut back to two leaves. As soon as the woody part has fully matured in autumn, to which end one heats the house during cool, cloudy autumn weather, one prunes the vine according to its strength back to 0.5–1 meter and stores it in a frost-free place for the winter. Of the side growths that appear in the following spring one leaves as many on the stock so that they are around 0.3 meter apart on each side. Later the spurs are pruned to 0.5 meter while leaving the end to grow unhindered in order

7 The editors were unable to determine the meaning of the phrase "stand im Bande," so it has been left untranslated.

to prune it again to 0.5–1 meter once the wood has matured. The spurs from which one could harvest some grapes in this summer are then

P. 58

pruned back to the first well-developed bud. Cutting is managed in the same way through successive years. When a gap appears in the vines by reason of old age or illness one cuts a spur, which had not borne fruit, from as low down as possible to a length of 0.5–1 meter and treats it in the same manner as the old stock, which is then cut out. Shortly before sprouting begins the soil is covered as far as the roots extend with a six-centimeter-thick layer of fresh cow or pig manure. In each successive year the old manure is removed and replaced with fresh. If, after several years, the soil is exhausted or some vines have rotten roots,

P. 59

the soil is partially replaced, which happens in the following manner: Along the back wall of the house, first a ditch of one-meter depth and 0.75 width is dug, while taking all possible care not to harm the roots that extend so far, and the earth thus excavated removed from the house. Thereafter the earth from the front wall of the ditch is carefully removed with forks and thrown behind or carried out—of course, one removes only the quantity of old earth that one wishes to replace with new; the remaining earth is piled up against the back wall of the house. The exposed roots are fixed with hooks to the surface in front of the ditch, sprayed with water and covered with raffia matting, so that

P. 60

they are protected against drying. In this manner the work continues until one has completely removed the vines with their roots undamaged. Now the old earth is mixed with the fresh good earth and the vines replanted after rotten roots have been cut out, namely so that the roots are evenly spread and close to the surface. Finally, the soil is covered with a five- to seven-centimeter-deep layer of fine horse manure to stop the soil on the surface drying out too quickly. This earth renewal is carried out frequently in England and, as both *Mr. Harrison* and other diligent vine forcers told me, always with exceptional success. For the second forcing,

P. 61

the house in Fig. G (No. 10 on the plan [ ]) is used.
In order to avoid treading the earth too hard during work there are, in each house as in this one, walkways Fig. G, a, constructed as shown in Fig. D. Where the space for walkways is too narrow, boards Fig. G, b are laid to be trodden upon. House No. 10 is, like all the other houses at *Knowsley,* built of

wood and namely it is so, as with all newer [houses], that they do not have movable windows but that the panes are mounted in thicker or thinner fixed frames. The top ventilation windows e are made as a piece. By means of this construction one saves a deal of money, and furthermore the house

P. 62

is much more tightly closed and retains the warmth much better than in houses with removable windows, and of course also much better than in houses with iron frames. The houses at *Knowsley* are never covered, but even when the outside temperature is -17 to -18°R, they retain the warmth so well that when the furnace is filled with coals at ten o'clock in the evening and the doors tightly closed there is no need to stoke the furnace again before six o'clock in the morning. With good quality paint these houses last a very long time. The heating equipment is as depicted in Figs. A and B; o in Fig. G are the hot-water pipes. Although there are pipes to heat the soil these are not used as soil heating has shown itself to be unfavorable

P. 63

to the health of the vines. With the apparatus d, whose lower part is shown from the front in Fig. K, it is possible to open the ventilation windows e along the entire house at the same time; the same happens with the lower ventilation windows by means of apparatus f.
Fig. I shows the plan of the latter apparatus; the iron rod i runs through the whole house and opens, when turned by f, all the front windows. Fig. L is the plan of house No. 10 with its heating pipe layout ($o-o^+$); the pipes o^{IIII} and o^+ serve to heat the peach house, No. 11 on the plan, attached to the grapevine house.
For second forcing, apart from the aforementioned varieties *Black Hamburgh*

P. 64

and *Foster's Seedling* the following are grown:
Madresfield Court, which variety seems better suited to second forcing than any other. The medium-sized bunches with large grapes have an exceptionally fine Muscat taste and a lovely reddish-brown color, but must be eaten very soon after a prolonged ripening as unfortunately they do not keep for long.
Royal Ascot with small bunches of very large black grapes,
Buckland Sweetwater, with large bunches of large, delicately light yellow grapes, is one of the best varieties for second forcing, but, like *Madresfield Court,* may not be pruned too short if one wishes to see perfect bunches.
Duke of Buccleuch, of which there were but a few young stocks in the *Knowsley Gardens,*

P. 65

which during my stay there bore no fruit but was highly praised by *Mr. Harrison* and others "for its beautiful, firm, very large amber-colored grapes of the finest aroma."

It may be remarked upon here that in England one uses the same houses for the same period every year for forcing, and thereby the stocks always have the same rest period. If one wishes to allow the stocks more rest after a particularly rich harvest then one leaves only a moderate number of bunches on the vine in the following year.

After the woody part has matured the stocks are pruned in the afore-mentioned manner around the beginning of October, at which time old loose bark is scraped off, and any

P. 66

holes and cracks filled with liquid grafting wax to prevent any pests from nesting there, the vines are thoroughly washed with brushes, namely with a solution of soap and salt in tobacco water. After this the stocks are painted with a thick paste composed of lime water with clay, sulphur, tobacco lye, soap, and soda in order to kill any remaining pests. Through spraying this mixture is washed off the trunks in the course of a few weeks.

After the stocks have been thus prepared, forcing begins around the middle of November. The surface of the earth is loosened and, after watering, covered with manure. As, namely, to ensure good maturation of the woody part the house has hitherto been kept dry,

P. 67

this makes thorough saturation of the soil necessary to start the forcing, and the water for this must be at a temperature of around 15°R. Saturation is repeated as needed every six to eight weeks; water at the required temperature is brought from the brewery (Plan: k.) in a large tank wagon.

Further treatment is set out in the description of the first forcing and analog to this, while of course the periods of sprouting, blooming, and maturing occur between fourteen days and three weeks later. Moist air is ensured by filling the basins on the hot pipes with water and by plentiful spraying; the constant humidity is not only necessary to promote growth but

P. 68

also to deter the dangerous red spider (*Acarus telarius*). If the latter appears, nevertheless, the house is sulphurated in that the heating pipes are coated in a paste of powdered sulphur in water and then made as hot as possible.

If there are vine varieties in the house whose grapes have a delicate skin then one may not sulphurate too heavily; House No. 5 was heavily sulphurated as the grapes began to color, and the grapes of *Foster's Seedling* and *Bucklands Sweetwater* got brown stripes and became unsightly, while *Black Hamburgh* was unaffected. As soon as the grapes are the size of peas the bunches are trimmed and the separate spurs tied apart. As soon as the grapes begin to color—around

P. 69

the middle of April—as much ventilation as possible is permitted. After the harvest, the house is kept as dry as possible. Temperatures in the first week of forcing are 10° during the day and 6°R at night, rising gradually through to the end of January to 13° in daytime and 10° at night, during February rising again to 16° in daytime and 13° at night. During flowering one keeps the house at 18° in the daytime and 10° at night, and after flowering one lets the temperature sink again to 14° in daytime and und 11° at night.

In house No. 7–8 on the plan, formerly consisting of two sections that have now been brought together, forcing begins at the beginning of January after preparation as described for No. 10. The temperature is initially the same

P. 70

as for second forcing and rises in the flowering period, i.e., mid-March, to 19° during the day and 17° at night. Varieties used for forcing here are:

Black Hamburgh,

Buckland Sweetwater,

Black Prince, large black grapes with a good taste, *Hamburgh Muscat,* similar to *Black Hamburgh* but with a fine Muscat taste bears plentiful, good bunches. For the fourth forcing, house No. 5 on the plan is used. Forcing begins in mid-February; the preparations for and methods of forcing correspond entirely to the aforementioned and the same applies to the later forcing houses. All houses are heated until the woody part of the vines reaches the desired stage. The following varieties are used for the fourth forcing:

P. 71

Ferdinand de Lesseps, with small white grapes, high yield,

Foster's Seedling

Buckland Sweetwater

Black Hamburg, in a very lovely variety with very dark, large grapes

House No. 6 is used for the next forcing, beginning in mid-March, and the varieties to be found there are:

Madresfield Court, began to rot immediately after ripening, and

Golden Champin[8] with very large grapes, large pretty dark yellow bunches of exceptional palatability; unfortunately the wood only matures in particularly favourable years;

Child of Hale, propagated from seed by the famous vintner *Meredith* in *Garston,* hardly differing from *Trebbiano,* a variety with fine large bunches

P. 72

of white hue and very faint taste.

Mrs. Pince, large bunches with medium-sized dark red grapes of a fine Muscat flavor.

Raisin de Calabre, very large white grapes, flavor not good,

Black Alicante, one of the most commendable varieties for late forcing, large bunches, large grapes, black, fine aroma, very palatable, keeps long after ripening.

Lady Downe's Seedling, with small bunches of very large grapes, black color, good flavor, also highly recommended.

Forcing starts in houses No. 1, 2, 3, 4, and 9 at the beginning of April.

In No. 1 the only variety is *Muscat of Alexandria,* a first-rate pale yellow very sweet Muscat grape of unsurpassable aroma; the grapes keep longer than any other

P. 73

variety. Mice are very fond of Muscat grapes, and therefore one places a piece of matting over each bunch with the rough side up. The mice do not like to touch the matting with their feet and the grapes remain untouched.

In No. 2, along with *Muscat of Alexandria* there is a young stock of *Dr. Hogg;* this is supposed to be a very good white variety with a Muscat flavor.

In No. 3 are:

Black Hamburgh, which, grafted onto *Lady Downe's,* bears a good yield,

Barbarossa, a very late black variety with exceptionally large bunches.

In No. 4 the following varieties are planted:

Black Hamburgh,

Champion Muscat, grafted on *Black Hamburgh,* with fine-looking red

P. 74

grapes. The same variety, grafted onto *Muscat of Alexandria,* produces even better, and *Duke of Buccleuch* too, grafted onto *Muscat of Alexandria,* is held to yield good harvests. Additionally:

Muscat Hamburgh

Madresfield Court

8 Jancke probably
   intended "champion."

Duke of Buccleuch.

In the year 1874 all the houses yielded a very rich harvest of large and well-formed grapes the like of which I have not yet seen on the Continent. No less results were achieved in the <u>peach forcing</u>.

For the same, houses 11 & 12 on the plan are used; No. 12, Fig. M is used for forcing first. Both houses are in general constructed like the grapevine house in Fig. G. The elevation is shown in Fig. H, part of the plan in Fig. L right. On each of the

P. 75

stronger rafters of the house an iron bracket (Fig. M, a) is fixed by the iron b. Through these brackets there run wires, about five millimeters thick, thirteen centimeters apart, serving to secure the trees. This iron espalier is not less than 0.5 meter from the glass, and because of this spacing the trees are more protected from the unfavorable influence of the weather—from being scorched in summer and chilled in winter—than is the case with espaliers that are too close to the glass.

On the back wall is also a wire espalier to support peach trees and these, too, produce good yields. The peach trees are trained in fan shape, which for them is the

P. 76

most natural and easiest form to train. The entire espalier is evenly covered with young wood and, in the ripening season, just as evenly with fruit. The older branches are, like the younger ones, straight, smooth, and healthy. Pruning, in the autumn, is restricted to removing branches where they have grown too densely. As soon as the terminal buds have formed in summer, that is, woody growth has stopped, the shoots are pinched out back to fifteen to twenty centimeters and water sprouts removed; the latter intervention is repeated several times.

Preparations for early forcing begin in mid-October. The trees are carefully cleaned after pruning. If whiteflies are found on the youngest shoots they are cleansed with a bristle brush and

P. 77

white spirit. The older branches are cleaned and painted with the same mixture as for grapevine growing. As soon as the coating has dried the trees are carefully bound with raffia so that the espalier is evenly covered and all branches are at the same distance from each other. In the first half of November the surface of the soil is loosened, the house thoroughly watered and the soil covered eight centimeters deep in cow manure. The house, which until now has been well ventilated, is then closed and forcing begun midth of November. The temperature in the first week is 8° during the day and 5°R at night and is raised through to the blossoming period that begins in mid-January, to 11° during the day and 9° at

P. 78

night. Shortly before the blossom appears the soil is once more thoroughly saturated, as the blossoms easily drop if the soil is too dry. From the beginning of forcing through to the opening of the blossom the trees are sprayed with lukewarm water twice a day, usually at nine o'clock in the morning and two o'clock in the afternoon, so that there is not a dry spot on any tree. During the blossom time constant humidity is achieved by means of frequent light spraying of the soil. Spraying the blossoms would have the consequence that through this contact with water the pollen grains swell so rapidly through endosmosis that the pollen tube bursts and its contents flow out through the wound instead of pushing through the pistil to the ovule. In order to achieve a full and general

P. 79

pollination, along with plentiful ventilation through the open windows one creates an artificial draft with a goose wing bound to a stick. Additionally, the temperature is not raised until the end of the blossom time in order to prolong the same and allow the blossom as much time as possible for pollination. After the blossom and through to stone formation, signified by a cessation of growth in the fruit, the temperatures are gradually raised to 13–14° in daytime and 12° at night. Spraying is once again extended to the trees. During stone formation the same temperatures are maintained. Now only so many fruits are brought on that in every square

P. 80

meter covered by a tree around ten fruits remain, as evenly distributed over the area as possible.

After stone formation watering is resumed. With the advent of more warmth spraying must also be repeated more often, as the green peach aphid appears as soon as the air is too dry. If it occurs despite all precautions the house is smoked out with tobacco paper; tobacco itself is too expensive in England to be used for this purpose. After stone formation through to the time when the fruit begins to color up, one raises the temperature little by little to 18° in the daytime and 16° at night. As soon as the fruit begins to color up, spraying the trees themselves ceases. During the ripening period, which commences around mid-May, one maintains the same temperatures but ventilates very fully and does not close the ventilation windows completely at night, as a constant stream of fresh air improves the flavor of the fruit immeasurably. The harvest in May of 1874 may be called a very good one.

Watering is carried out as and when needed; at *Knowsley* the peach houses are saturated four to five times during the year. For early forcing the following varieties are used:

1. Peach:

Royal George (Madeleine à petites fleurs) bore large quantities of fine, juicy and flavorsome fruit and is in any case one of the best varieties for early forcing,

Bellegarde is the second variety to ripen, also an excellent forcing variety of great

flavor, with small blossoms and large fruit, and keeps for longer after picking than most of the others,

Violette hâtive, likewise good for forcing, with large, attractive, and sound fruit,

Burrington, a worthy equal of the three aforementioned with regard to both fecundity and the flavor of the fruits. Additionally, a young *Dagmar* tree is to be found in the house, the sort of which is also highly commended for forcing.

2. Nectarines:

Hunts' Tanny is the first of the nectarines to ripen, bears plentiful fruit with flesh that detaches easily from the stone, becomes mealy soon after ripening and must therefore be used quickly.

Elruge, likewise with flesh that detaches from the stone, is one of the best nectarines and eminently suitable for forcing,

Violette hâtive, likewise highly recommended in every respect for forcing, with flesh that detaches from the stone,

Impératrice, detaching flesh, good, flavorsome, very good for forcing.

For the second peach forcing, house No. 11 on the plan is used, which is constructed like No. 12 (Fig. M). The second forcing begins around the middle of January after preparations following those of the first forcing, which is completed in December. The treatment is on the whole the same as for the first forcing. Blossoms appear in early February and the fruit ripens in June. Varieties used for the second

forcing are the following:
Royal George
Bellegarde
Violette hâtive
Barrington
These four can be recommended for the second forcing just as well as for the first.
Grosse Mignonne, very good for forcing, bears plentiful, large, and very fine tasting fruit,
Noblesse bears numerous, very large, pale fruit, which may be said to surpass all other varieties in taste.
Of the nectarines, there may be found in the house:
Elruge
Violette hâtive
Impératrice, which produces plentiful and good harvests by the second forcing as well.

For <u>fig forcing</u>, house No. 25 on the plan is used; Figure N shows a cross-section, Figure

O, 2 the plan of the same (Fig. O, 1 is the plan of the cherry house).
By means of two levers (Fig. N, k), located at both ends of the house, the front windows are opened, and likewise the upper windows are opened by two lever mechanisms. At the front of the house stand two rows of fig trees. The back wall, with espaliers, is almost entirely covered by two fig trees trained in fan shapes. Throughout the summer the fig trees receive plentiful water. Weak shoots are cut out. The fruits that form by the end of July are broken off as they would not develop well; those which appear on the tree later are left to grow, they are the first to ripen.

Preparations for forcing begin in December. Straw remnants from the previous year's manure layer are removed, the trees are cleansed of the annually occurring mealy bug (*Coccus adonidum L.*) with a bristle brush and white spirit and then scrubbed with rough brushes and tobacco lye in which soap and soda are dissolved.
Once this is completed all holes and cracks in the old trunks are sealed with *Mastic L'homme Lefort,* as they serve as breeding places for pests. For this the entire trees, with the exception of the youngest shoots, are coated with the

aforementioned mixture. Once the coating is completely dry the branches of the trees that grow too close to the glass are

P. 87

tied down with strong twine, so that some trees almost give the impression of "weeping" trees. This binding down should also promote fruiting; those branches that grow too close to each other are tied apart so that all are as equally spaced as possible.

In the first half of January the soil surface in the fig house is loosened, namely very lightly and carefully in order not to damage the roots of the fig trees, most of which lie very close to the surface. The soil is then thoroughly saturated and thereafter covered with a five- to seven-centimeter-deep layer of firm cow manure,

P. 88

whereupon the forcing begins.

The temperature of the house is then initially kept at 9° during the day and 7° at night, the evaporating pans on the hot-water pipes kept filled and the tree sprayed twice daily, morning and afternoon, from all sides with lukewarm water. The temperature of the house is gradually raised through to the end of March to 16° during the day and 14° at night, and spraying repeated more often as the heat increases. As far as the weather allows the house is ventilated, as fine-tasting fruit may only be achieved with plentiful ventilation.

When the sun shines one no longer sprays the leaves, as they would promptly go bad, but only the soil

P. 89

and the trunks. Watering must be repeated from time to time, as fig trees require a great deal of water during their growth period. From April onward the soil is not given much moisture as an excess of the same gives the fruit, as it approaches ripeness, a watery taste and often causes them to burst; notwithstanding this one may not allow the air to become too dry but, by means of frequent light spraying, retain the necessary humidity.

From April until the ripening period, which commences at the beginning of May, the temperature is raised once again to 17° during the day and 15° at night; when the sun shines it can, as with every forcing,

P. 90

rise by another 5°, and during overcast and cold weather be 2–3° less. In mid-June a second picking is made. After the picking the house is ventilated as much as possible and copiously watered. The varieties used for forcing at *Knowsley* are as follows:

Brown Turkey is one of the most suitable varieties for forcing and produces an enormous yield of finely colored, extremely tasty fruit.
White Marseilles, likewise good for forcing, ripens early, very sweet,
Carte Kennedy, with large, very sweet fruit, produced a very good yield.

The house used for <u>cherry forcing</u> is built in the same way as the fig house but does not have so many heating pipes, as the cherries

P. 91

do not need such intense heat as the figs. While every cubic meter of the cherry house has only approx. 8.3 square decimeters of heating pipe surface, in the fig house 14.7 square decimeters are calculated for a cubic meter.
The plan of the cherry house with its pipes is drawn in Fig. O1. The cross section is like that of the fig house except that two pipes are omitted, and in the space before the paths stand three rows of trees instead of two.
Against the back wall stand fan-trained cherry trees of the following varieties:
Transparent, very flavorsome with a transparent skin, does not bear very heavily,
Black Tartarian bears good, large black fruit in great numbers,

P. 92

Bigarreau, white, delicious, heavy yield.
In the front part of the house stand:
May Duke, the best for forcing, bears very gratifyingly
Black Eagle, delicious,
Reine Hortense produces large red fruit but in no great numbers.
After one has given the cherry trees as much air as possible and watered them often, now and again with dissolved manure, through the summer and autumn, at the end of December the surface of the soil is loosened, but very carefully as the roots lie as shallow as those of the figs. After a thorough saturation the surface is covered with cow manure. The cherry trees were not washed or painted, as no pests occur on the same. One does not begin forcing until

P. 93

the beginning of January because earlier forcing, with the rarity of sunshine at the end of winter, would make good fruiting dubious. The temperature starts at 8° during the day and 4° at night, and the trees are thoroughly sprayed with lukewarm water each day, once or twice depending on the weather. The house is plentifully ventilated as far as the weather allows.

Through to the blossom time, which begins in the first half of February, the temperature is raised to 10° in the daytime and 8° at night. Artificial pollination is not carried out.

Spraying the trees is suspended during the blossom time, but the necessary humidity is maintained by watering the soil. During the blossom time one must

P. 94

allow the trees as much fresh air as possible. After blossoming has ceased the entire tree is once more sprayed and the temperature gradually raised to 15° in the daytime and 12° at night through to ripening. During the period of stone formation the young branches of the trees are not sprayed, neither do they receive heavy watering. As soon as the fruit begins to color up the trees are no longer sprayed and nets are placed over the ventilation windows to make it impossible for sparrows to enter. (The cherry trees standing along the wall of the kitchen garden are also covered with nets as soon as they begin to color up.)

Ripening begins in April. The yield in 1874 was relatively good.

P. 95

For pineapple forcing at *Knowsley* a house has been built in two sections; Fig. P is a cross section, Fig. R the plan, and Fig. Q an elevation of part of the house. Fig. S is the section of the pipes a in Fig. R, the pipe b is likewise arranged, with c and d there are no sliders e, e by means of which one can shut off, with a and b, the hot water from the cooler part of the house as necessary.

Young pineapple plants are gained from the old ones after they have borne their last fruit by allowing the strongest shoot between the leaves to grow but cutting off the others, likewise removing the part of the old plant above the shoot

P. 96

and dusting the wounds with charcoal powder to prevent rotting. The old plants stand in the house until February and are kept dry through the winter. At the end of February the box behind the pineapple house is filled with manure and dead leaves, so that after the manure has subsided its surface is 0.6 meter from the glass. The box is about two meters deep. The young shoots or layers are at the same time removed from the mother plant, carefully freed of their lower leaves and planted in sixteen-centimeter-wide pots in a mixture of clayey lawn earth with a small addition of crumbly heath earth and sand. Once the temperature of the

P. 97

manure has sunk to 22°R, around fourteen days after the bed has been laid, the manure is covered with a two or three ^{dcm} deep layer of tanbark and the layers set into this at 0.5 meter from each other.

Immediately after planting the layers are lightly watered, thereafter they are not heavily watered until the roots begin to develop, something which may be easily determined as new leaves develop in the heart. Thereafter they are given lukewarm water every three to five days as necessary. In the first weeks after the plants are set the box is only ventilated a little, and only to let out the vapors arising from

P. 98

the manure. As long as night frosts are to be expected the bed is covered at night with straw matting. During the summer the bed is ventilated daily but moderately, and in very hot weather lightly shaded; the plants are also sprayed daily with lukewarm water. From time to time liquid manure (prepared from deer dung) is added to the water. In November the young plants are set, at half their height, in the beds filled with leaves in the cooler section of the pineapple house; through the winter the plants are not kept too moist.

The temperature is initially set at 13° during the day, 10°R at night and is gradually raised through until May

P. 99

to 18° in the daytime and 15° at night.

From February onward one begins to spray the plants again and, by watering the walls and paths, to make the air moist. At the beginning of May the young plants are potted up in twenty-five- to thirty-centimeter pots, in the same mixture as before. Through the summer the house is very well ventilated and sprayed, the plants watered with a manure solution and the temperature raised through until July to 21° in the daytime and 18° at night.

(In the following winter one lowers the temperature again to 12–13° and keeps the plants very dry).

In September the pineapple plants, which have grown strongly through the summer,

P. 100

are replanted in slightly larger pots and brought into the freshly laid leaf beds of the warm section so that each has plenty of space (around one meter from each other). The plants are watered once only and then kept completely dry until January. The temperature throughout this period is 13° by day and 10°R by night. The air is kept dry and carefully renewed by means of the ventilation system.

Once the plants have been rested for a few months one begins to force them at the end of January; they are watered with lukewarm water and the temperature in the house is raised. As soon as the plants begin to put out new leaves and the old leaves spread,

P. 101

one begins to spray them with lukewarm water again. During the blossoming period spraying is suspended. Once blossoming ceases one recommences abundant spraying and frequent watering at 20–30°R; about once a week a fertilizer solution is applied.

Through to ripening, the temperature is raised to 22° in the daytime and 20° at night.

As soon as the fruit approaches ripeness, watering is reduced. The plants at *Knowsley* last year were very healthy and, with the exception of four, completely free of pests. These said plants, as soon as pineapple scale (*Coccus bromeliae*) was detected, were removed from the house and their fruit ripened

P. 102

in a dung heap.

The varieties cultivated at *Knowsley* are as follows:

Black Jamaica, with dark brown-green fruit, which takes on a lighter yellow color as it ripens; it is considered one of the most rewarding and flavorsome varieties, fruit egg-shaped,

Smooth leaved Cayenne, has leaves without spikes and large fruit that are as broad above as below, is held to have a similarly good aroma, apart from these *Montserrat,* further, diverse varieties of *Queen* that are also to be recommended, *White Providence,* with large but not very fine fruit.

For melon forcing at *Knowsley* the following varieties are used:

Malvern Hall is one of the best for forcing,

P. 103

the fruit is ribbed, the flesh red,

Victory of Bath, with long elliptical fruit, is cut before reaching its full ripeness, *Colston Basset,* likewise a good forcing variety with ribbed fruit and white flesh, *Trentham hybrid,* a highly commended lightly ribbed net melon, long, with pale yellow flesh, bears very early and is cultivated both in glasshouses and in the open. *Dr. Hogg,* with thick-skinned, pure yellow, ribbed, almost spherical fruit, *Conqueror* is the earliest net melon, with large three- to four-pound heavy, ribbed fruit,

Incomparable is a very good ribbed net melon with green flesh.

For forcing, house No. 13 on the plan is used, the which is constructed similarly to the cucumber house (Fig. A) but is markedly smaller. Additionally, melons are grown on the cultivated land behind the kitchen garden, namely using the cloche method very common in France.

For forcing, at the beginning of January the first melons are sown in pots and put in the grapevine house, No. 23 on the plan. For the first propagation from seed one uses the *Conqueror* variety.

As soon as the pots have been placed in the grapevine house they are surrounded with wire netting and covered to keep off mice and snails. As soon as the pots are full of roots and the

plants have three to four leaves, the which happens in mid-February, they are planted out in the beds prepared for them in the melon house. Preparations comprise filling the beds with firmly trodden-down leaves and manure in January, after about fourteen days one adds a five-centimeter layer of clay mixed with partially rotted manure. Beneath the middle of each window a pile of the same mixture, about fifteen centimeters high and thirty centimeters wide, is made and one melon plant set in each. One then showers the mounds frequently with lukewarm water, and a manure solution is applied twice a week. As soon as the roots have spread through the mound

and are showing their tips outside it, the mound is covered with a new layer of the same mixture, and this is repeated until the bed is fairly evenly filled.

The temperature in the house during the first week of forcing is 17°R during the day and 15° at night, and is gradually raised through to ripening, which commences in mid-May, to 20° during the day and 18° at night. As soon as the plants have put out six to seven leaves they are trimmed so that two tendrils are created, each of which is secured by a stake and trained onto the espalier twenty centimeters from the windowpanes.

Air is introduced daily from the commencement of forcing, more or less depending on the weather,

increasing from the ripening period onward.

As soon as the plants are in bloom, a fine paintbrush is used to transfer the pollen from the male to the female blooms. When the fruits become larger one lays them on boards, one end of which lies on an espalier wire and the other fixed with twine to the next-higher wire.

Cultivation of the later varieties is generally the same.

For growing outdoors *Trentham hybrid* is used. One throws up a meter-high embankment with a gentle southern slope. On this embankment, after it has been covered with five centimeters

P. 108

of short, partially rotted horse manure, the young plants are set in April when they have put out three to four leaves, spaced one meter from each other. They are covered with glass bells (cloches), which are covered on cool nights with old raffia matting.

The cloches are gradually ventilated more freely by laying pieces of wood under them and eventually completely removed so that the plants can spread over the south-facing slope. Care for the same is similar to that in the glasshouse.

In France one lays out the embankments running from north to south and allows, of the two tendrils, one to lie on the east and one on the west side.

P. 109

For <u>cucumber forcing</u>, house No. 22 on the plan is used, of which Fig. A1 is a cross section, and Figure B the plan.

The previous year at *Knowsley* only *Rollisons Telegraph* was grown as one of the best forcing cucumbers. The cucumbers grow fifty to sixty centimeters long, remain almost straight, and have a fine taste. Sowing out happens in the second half of August in pots, set in a manure bed.

At the beginning of October, when the plants have put out three to four leaves, they are brought into the cucumber house. The beds are already filled some weeks before with leaves and manure, and after the

P. 110

temperature has begun to sink, covered with a twenty-centimeter-deep layer consisting of clay, leaf mold, and rotted horse manure from old mushroom beds.

At the beginning of October the earth is raked up so that piles were 1.5 meters from each other. A cucumber is planted in each pile and, as soon as the roots begin to spread, the piles are covered with earth of the same mixture.

In the blossoming period one pollinates with a paintbrush at midday. The temperature of the house is kept fairly constant at 20°R during the day and 17° at night and the plants fairly plentifully watered, namely, when the fruit

P. 111

swells. The first fruits are picked in December, the last in May. After the harvest the plants are removed, the bed freshly laid and planted with new cucumbers.

For the cultivation of <u>beans</u> no special house has been erected at *Knowsley*; rather, one uses the edges of beds and the window ledge in the pineapple house, the boxes behind the same house as long as they are available, and the melon house. Varieties of bean used for forcing are:

Williams's and *Osborne's*, both of which grow very low and produce a plentiful crop, albeit of rather small beans. Following the harvest of beans grown outdoors, those

P. 112

in the bed in front of houses Nos. 10 to 12 are sown in early September in a semi-cold manure bed, and subsequently every fourteen days sowing in pots of twenty-five-centimeter diameter. The pots are half-filled with loose manure bed earth and one lays ten beans in a circle, about five centimeters from the edge and four centimeters deep. These pots are stood in the melon house, where the temperature from November to January is maintained at 16° during the day 14° at night; watering is kept sparse.

As soon as the plants have a few leaves the pots are topped up with manure bed earth to two-thirds of their depth and taken over to the pineapple house, where they find their place upon the side

P. 113

windowsills and the margins of beds contained in red sandstone paving stones. The plants are supported by inserting broom twigs.

The latest sowing is always placed in the warmest place in the melon house. Picking follows around two months after sowing.

In January, when the melon house is being prepared to receive the melons, one prepares a manure bed for the following beans, fills it with a fifteen-centimeter layer of manure bed earth and rakes this together so that a long mound from beneath the center of each window stretches from the front to the back wall. Two rows of beans are planted on each of these long mounds. Ventilation

P. 114

depends on the weather conditions; if the weather is bright the plants are sprayed, but not during the blossoming period.

After a few weeks more boxes are laid out with manure and planted, until beans can be planted outdoors.

For <u>strawberry forcing</u> at *Knowsley* there is likewise no special house; they are, like the beans, grown as a side product in other houses.

For forcing, in August sturdy runners are planted in a well-prepared bed and carefully tended through to the winter.

In winter the bed is covered with short-rotted horse manure, and in April
of the following year the best plants are potted up in a mixture of leaf mold

P. 115

and manure bed earth, and placed along the kitchen garden paths, carefully
watered, and bad leaves and runners pinched out. In July they are planted out
and left in their place until being taken into the respective glasshouses for forcing.
In late autumn, when the cold weather arrives, they are covered with leaves.
For the first forcing *Black Prince* is used; this variety bears plentiful small fruit
of middling flavor.
The pots are taken into the pineapple house in mid-October, where they are
placed on two of the shelves above the central path (cf. Fig. P).
For the second forcing one uses *Keen's Seedling,*

P. 116

one of the best forcing strawberries; for the pots there is a shelf against the
back wall of the second grapevine house (cf. Fig. G).
In the fig house there are shelves above the ways for the third forcing, and in
the cherry house for the fourth; the former is conducted with *Duc de Malakoff,*
and for the latter one chooses *Oscar* and *Heywood prolific*; all three varieties are
worthy of recommendation.
After them, *President* with its large, fine fruit is grown in the grapevine house
No. 6 on the plan, followed by *Sir Charles Napier* in grapevine houses Nos. 1
and 2 on the plan, and the last forcing uses *Dr. Hogg,* one of the most attractive
and best strawberries: the pots are stood in the cherry house and the fig house
after *Duc de Malakoff, Heywood prolific,* and *Oscar* have been harvested.

P. 117

<u>Vegetable growing</u> at *Knowsley* is in general the same as here. Rhubarb is grown
in great quantities for the leafstalk, as is celery, whereby one binds the leaves
together to produce blanched, very tasty, young leafstalks to be enjoyed with
salt without further preparation, and customarily together with watercress and
mustard, the latter of which one sows every eight to fourteen days in boxes in
order to have young plants all through the winter.
<u>Mushroom growing</u> does not differ from ours at home. In the farm building
i on the plan there is a closed dark room in which there are four mushroom
beds, each about ten meters in length; they

P. 118

are filled in turn from autumn through to spring with fresh horse manure that
one packs firmly with a roller. When the manure has cooled down to around

22°R, the spawn is raked into the surface of the bed, and as soon as the manure is filled with the mycelium (after about ten days) a mixture of leaves and lawn earth is spread five centimeters deep on the bed and pressed lightly. Through to the emergence of the young mushrooms the bed is periodically sprayed with lukewarm water.

On my return journey from England to Germany I stayed, as on the outward journey, in London for a few days in order to visit the famous *Kew Gardens* with the splendid, extensive museums, the beautiful great Palm House,

P. 119

the incomparable fern collection, etc., and also to visit the large establishments of *Veitch, Bull, Williams,* and *Henderson* again.

Unfortunately my time was too short to look around the aforementioned establishments and the botanic garden with its rich plant treasures as fully as I would have liked. Nevertheless I had numerous opportunities to make highly interesting notes about plant care and cultivation, the propagation and distribution of useful plants (in the *Kew Museum*), etc., and to see cultivated plants of all species in an extraordinary perfection, along with many large and fine examples of novelties, of which to

P. 120

conclude I wish to mention a few:
Allocasia Marshalli
   "   *illustris,* both are similar to *A. Jenningsii* but *A. Marshalli* has markedly larger leaves, while *illustris* differs from *A. Jenningsii* in a silver-gray patch in the center of the leaf. Of *Anthurium Scherzerianum album* I saw a very striking example at *William's,* which however was not blooming when I was there.
Croton limbatum, the dark green leaves have a dark yellow central rib, similarly colored patches and reddish-yellow edges.
Croton majesticum has narrow very long leaves, the younger ones are yellow, and the older ones red.
Croton spirale, with corkscrew-shaped leaves.

P. 121

Croton volutum with colorful leaves that roll back on themselves, less beautiful than extraordinary.
Curculigo recurvata striala, of the habitus of the common *C. r.,* the leaves have white stripes in the direction of the veins.
Cyrtanthera chryostephana with beautiful golden-yellow blooms.

Dioscorea illustrata has large leaves that are a fine green flecked with silver-gray above and red beneath.

Hibiscus puniceus with large luminous carmine red blooms,

Hibiscus miniatus semiplenus, likewise very lovely,

Kentia Canterburyana, a very elegant Palm.

Macrozamia cylindrica,

   "   *corallipes,*

   "   *plumosa.*

The last mentioned is probably one of the most beautiful Cycads.

P. 122

Maranta Mackoyana is found in England, as in Belgium already, as very large and fine examples, likewise:

Maranta hieroglyphica

Maranta Semanni has lovely velvety green leaves with a lighter central rib, the underside red,

Musa Africana, with red leafstalks,

Pandanus Veitchii, exceeding *P. Javanicus var.* by far in beauty,

Poinsettia pulcherrima with the luminous red crown of leaves surrounding the blooms, easily propagated from cuttings,

Pteris serrulata cristata variegata,

Spathiphyllum pictum, with very finely marked leaves.

ex horto
DUMBARTON OAKS TEXTS
IN GARDEN AND LANDSCAPE STUDIES

Dumbarton Oaks Research Library and Collection, Washington, D.C.

Ex horto is devoted to classic works on the philosophy, art, and techniques of landscape design. Augmented with contemporary scholarly commentary, the series offers historical texts from numerous languages and reintroduces valuable works long out of print. The volumes cover a broad geographical and temporal range, from ancient Chinese poetry to twentieth-century German treatises, and constitute a library of historical sources that have defined the core of the field. By making these works newly available, the series provides unprecedented access to the foundational literature of garden and landscape studies.

Further information on Garden and Landscape Studies publications can be found at www.doaks.org/publications.

Garden Culture of the Twentieth Century
    Leberecht Migge, author; and David H. Haney, editor and translator

Travel Report: An Apprenticeship in the Earl of Derby's Kitchen Gardens and Greenhouses at Knowsley, England
    Hans Jancke, author; Joachim Wolschke-Bulmahn, editor;
    and Mic Hale, translator